C000022799

Visual Basic

PROGRAMMER'S REFERENCE

Dan Rahmel

Osborne **McGraw-Hill**

Berkeley ▪ New York ▪ St. Louis ▪ San Francisco
Auckland ▪ Bogotá ▪ Hamburg ▪ London
Madrid ▪ Mexico City ▪ Milan ▪ Montreal
New Delhi ▪ Panama City ▪ Paris ▪ São Paulo
Singapore ▪ Sydney ▪ Tokyo ▪ Toronto

Osborne **McGraw-Hill**
2600 Tenth Street
Berkeley, California 94710
U.S.A.

For information on translations or book distributors outside the U.S.A., or to
arrange bulk purchase discounts for sales promotions, premiums, or
fund-raisers, please contact Osborne/**McGraw-Hill** at the above address.

Visual Basic: Programmer's Reference

Publisher   Brandon A. Nordin
Editor-in-Chief   Scott Rogers
Acquisitions Editor   Megg Bonar
Project Editor   Claire Splan
Editorial Assistant   Gordon Hurd, Stephane Thomas
Technical Editor   Greg Guntle
Copy Editor   Jan Jue
Proofreader   Joe Sadusky
Computer Designer   Michelle Galicia, Peter F. Hancik
Illustrator   Sue Albert
Series Design   Peter F. Hancik

:34567890 DOC DOC 901987654321098

ISBN 0-07-882458-3

I would like to dedicate this book to the unsung heroes at Microsoft who, though much maligned, have produced an Insanely Great family of programming products.

About the Author

Dan Rahmel is a Visual Basic programmer with over 12 years of experience designing and implementing information systems and deploying mid-sized client/server systems using Visual Basic and Visual FoxPro. He has co-authored several books, including *Developing Client-Server Applications with Visual Basic* and *Special Edition Visual Basic for Applications 5* and is a regular contributor to *DBMS, Internet Advisor*, and *American Programmer* magazines.

CONTENTS @ A GLANCE

CONTENTS

viii Contents

xii   Contents

xvi   Contents

ACKNOWLEDGMENTS

Writing this book has been extremely enjoyable due to the contents of the book itself and the people I had the pleasure of working with. I often have wanted just this book, organized with quick examples and a powerful index. So as I worked on it, I had the selfish pleasure of knowing it was something I could use almost daily.

Combining the creation of the book itself with the superior Osborne staff often made the difficult seem easy. I'd like to thank the people on the Osborne staff that I interacted with often (Megg Bonar, Claire Splan, and Jan Jue) and all the others who had to work tirelessly in production and editing to produce the book.

I'd like to thank my parents (Ron and Marie), siblings (David and Darlene), and friends (David Rahmel, Greg Mickey, Ted Ehr, Ed Gildred, Juan Leonffu, Weld O'Connor, Don Murphy) for their tireless support.

Most of all, I'd like to thank the reader. By buying this book, you make it possible for all of us in the book industry to labor to produce good work. When pulling the long hours to complete a book, knowing that every little improvement will help your audience is what really makes the difference. Thanks.

INTRODUCTION

Welcome to the *Visual Basic Programmer's Reference*. This book contains reference information for the Visual Basic/VBA/VB Script family of products. The book generally assumes some programming experience, but if you're new to programming, you will most likely find this book invaluable. I have tried to provide extensive cross-references within the book. Therefore, if you know the general type of functionality you need, following the See Also references, index, or other aids will lead you to your exact topic. For any reference book, an introduction is crucially important because this is typically the only place in the book where a reader will actually sit and read. The rest of the time spent with a reference book is usually for quick lookup. The Introduction sets the tone for how the book can be used. I have written this book with the idea of making it extremely usable for programming projects. The most unique feature of this book is the Immediate Window examples provided with each reference command. Seldom does a programmer want to know about a Visual Basic command for random curiosity. I want to know how to use the command, so I constructed the book with this philosophy in mind. With each term is an example that can be entered and executed immediately.

The second best feature of the book is the object diagrams in Part III. Object diagrams provided by Microsoft and replicated in most other books show a jumble of objects and collections. It is often difficult to tell which shape in the diagram denotes a single object versus a collection. Not so in my diagrams. Each diagram shows only a single level of the object model. Collections are obvious both by their appearance (like a deck of stacked cards) and the listing of the plural collection name followed by the singular object name shown below in parentheses. I hope that you find these object models an invaluable reference when creating Visual Basic/VBA projects. Object models are becoming almost more important to a project than the actual programming language. For this reason, any improvements that can be made in understanding and referencing the object model (whether it's for Excel, PowerPoint, or any system) should be embraced.

The index was created to be as thorough as possible, but everyone looks up topics in a different way. If you don't find something listed under the heading you expected, please make a note of it and send us the information. That way, the next revision of the book can be even better.

I hope you find this book as useful as the people at Coherent Data already have. I also hope you'll provide feedback with any suggestions you have or mistakes you find. We have a page on our Web site dedicated to taking your suggestions. Please stop by.

Part I
Overview of VB, VBA, and VB Script

Basic has been evolving for almost 30 years. Today, while much of the code that was written on earlier versions of Basic (such as MS-Basic, AppleSoft, Qbasic, QuickBasic, and so on) will execute with very little modification, line numbers and Goto statements of the past have been mostly discarded for the subroutine/function model currently used.

There are approximately 250 commands and functions available in the Visual Basic language. The language also supports object-oriented programming access through the use of dot (.) commands to navigate the object hierarchy. Visual Basic, for good reason, does not support multiple inheritance as other languages such as C++ do. Visual Basic object programs are far easier to understand and debug.

In the near future, the Visual Basic language itself will probably change little. Microsoft has been expanding the functionality on the Visual Basic systems primarily through more robust objects (see Part III). In fact, some functions that used to be included in the language itself have been moved into a particular object (such as the Err object).

Differences Among the Languages

Visual Basic and Visual Basic for Applications (VBA) use the same central language engine. The differences between the two languages are extremely minor, such as the lack of a LoadPicture command in VBA. The only commands missing between the two implementations are those based on the environment that they run within.

VB Script varies greatly from the other Visual Basic programming languages. VB Script, a subset of Visual Basic, is small, simple, and easy to port to various machine implementations and microprocessors. Because VB Script code needs to download in real time across a network, whether on a web page or within an Outlook/Exchange form, security is another primary consideration.

VB Script, therefore, lacks some commands that might be difficult to implement in various environments (such as the Timer command) and functions that could be accomplished by use of other means (trimming the number of string functions, for example). It also leaves out all disk-access capabilities. For a complete list of commands that are missing from the VB Script language, see the "VB Script Missing Commands" section later in this part of the book.

Three Development Systems

Visual Basic is now available across a broad range of development systems. The standardization of the Visual Basic 5.0 engine has done a great deal to give the various Visual Basic and Visual Basic for Applications (VBA) implementations similar features and appearances.

Visual Basic Environment

The Visual Basic environment is a complete development environment, with form designer, tool palettes, debugger, and project-management capabilities. If you are unfamiliar with the Visual Basic environment, I recommend that you purchase one of the many fine books on learning Visual Basic. Microsoft has made the Visual Basic and VBA environments in their current implementations resemble each other.

If you're just beginning to learn Visual Basic, there are excellent books on the market, such as *Teach Yourself Visual Basic* by Bob Albrecht and Karl Albrecht (Osborne/McGraw-Hill, 1996) or *Visual Basic 5 from the Ground Up* by Gary Cornell (Osborne/McGraw-Hill, 1997). These books will teach you the basics of the programming language and the general Visual Basic system. Learning Visual Basic will make moving to VBA a simple step.

Visual Basic and VBA differ most not in their language implementations, which are nearly identical, but in the controls included with the system. Figure 1-1 shows all of the controls that are included by default in the Visual Basic Control palette.

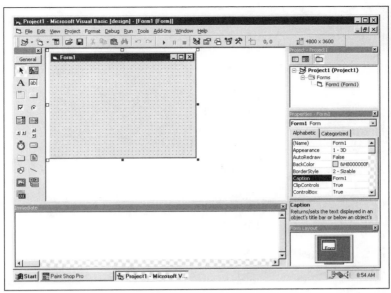

Figure 1-1.   Visual Basic Control palette

Table 1-1 shows each control icon by name. These are only the
components of the simplified palette. This palette does not include
other controls included with the Visual Basic system, such as the
Windows Custom Controls (tab strips, toolbars, clocks, and so on),
data-access controls (data-aware grid control, data-aware list box,
and so on), and extra user-interface components.

You might notice that the two most prominent inclusions in the
Visual Basic palette that are missing from the VBA palette are the
DataControl and the Timer items. Graphical data access in VBA
applications must be done with direct coding to the Data Access
Objects (see the appropriate section in Part III) or through
Microsoft Access.

Time-based applications in VBA must use the Timer function to
manually monitor time progression. Although both languages
feature the Timer function, the Timer control included with Visual
Basic will execute autonomously at given intervals. Using the
Timer control dramatically simplifies applications that must have
events occur at specific time periods.

Control	Name
A	Label
	Frame
	Checkbox
	ComboBox
	HScrollbar
	Timer
	DirListBox
	Shape
	Image
	OLEControl
	PictureBox
	TextBox
	CommandButton
	OptionButton
	ListBox
	Vscrollbar
	DriveListBox
	FileListBox
	Line
	DataControl

Table 1-1.   Visual Basic controls

Most operations in the Visual Basic environment have a keyboard equivalent. Table 1-2 lists the key codes for frequently used operations.

Visual Basic for Applications Environment

The Visual Basic for Applications environment provides a complete project-based development system for creating VBA applications. Figure 1-2 displays the environment that may be accessed by pressing ALT-F11 in Excel, Word, PowerPoint, or Project. It is also available under the Macro menu. Access 97 contains its own specialized environment that mirrors VBA but includes special features for database access.

The left window in the VBA environment shows the current Project window. The *Project* window displays all of the current open documents. Within the documents may exist objects, modules, user forms, and references. If a macro is recorded, it is either added to the document itself or to a code module. The figure shows a single module, NewMacros, created in Word automatically by recording a macro.

Double-clicking on a module item will display a Code window. The *Code* window displays all of the code associated with a module or a user form. The two combo boxes displayed at the top of the window determine what procedure is shown in the window. The left combo box is used to select the current object (forms, control, and so on), or it can be set to "(General)" for the general

Key	Description
F2	Object Browser
F4	Show properties
F5	Compile and execute
CTRL-F5	Start with full compile
F8	Step into
SHIFT-F8	Step over
F9	Set breakpoint
SHIFT-F9	Quick watch
CTRL-G	Show Immediate window

Table 1-2.   Frequently Used Key Codes

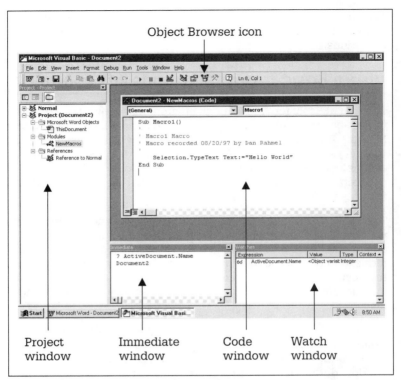

Object Browser icon

Project window

Immediate window

Code window

Watch window

Figure 1-2. VBA programming environment

procedures not attached to a specific object. Since a code module has no objects, the window will always display "(General)" in a module. The right combo box is used to select the procedure or event code to be shown in the actual window.

The gray area to the left of the Code window will show any current breakpoint and the position of the current execution line when VBA is in the debugging mode (also called the break mode). Clicking in the gray area next to a code line will set a breakpoint on that line. A red bullet will appear in the area to identify a set breakpoint.

At the bottom of the screen, you'll notice the *Immediate* window. This window is one of the most powerful aspects of the VBA system because it allows entry of nearly any Visual Basic command for immediate execution. This allows you to test small parts of code and new commands and immediately see the results. I have included Immediate window examples throughout this book. Each example demonstrates a fundamental aspect of the specific command, function, property, or method.

The *Watch* window is used to display information on particular variables. For debugging purposes, the Watch window can be used to consistently examine a small set of variables. Changes can be viewed as they take place. *Conditional* watches, which will cause a break to occur when the variable reaches a particular value, may also be set.

Adding a user form to a project will display the Form construction window and the Control palette, shown in Figure 1-3. Any controls available on the Control palette may be inserted into the form. (See Table 1-3 for the names of the VBA controls.) Additional controls that may be available to the VBA system but that are not currently on the palette may be added by clicking the right mouse button in an unused area of the palette.

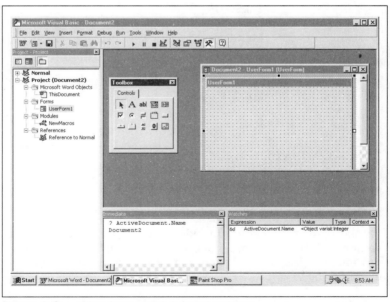

Figure 1-3.   VBA forms and Control palette

Control	Name
A	Label
ab|	TextBox
▣	ComboBox
▣	ListBox
☑	Checkbox
⊙	OptionButton
⇄	ToggleButton
⊡	Frame
⌐	CommandButton
⊡	TabStrip
⊡	MultiPage
▤	Scrollbar
▤	SpinButton
🖼	Image

Table 1-3.   VBA controls

What Can't VBA Do?

With all of the new features included in VBA, people often wonder what extra capabilities are provided by the complete Visual Basic environment. Visual Basic offers significant additional features enabling you to

- Compile an EXE (although there is a Microsoft Access run time now available)

1

- Create ActiveX DLLs (required for use when creating Active Server components and for use with Microsoft Transaction Server)
- Create database tools such as the Data Manager
- Create OLE Automation servers
- Create ActiveX Documents (which are actually Visual Basic applications that can be automatically deployed and installed on a client machine through the web)
- Create ActiveX Controls
- Increase execution speed because Visual Basic is fully compiled (although you cannot create a stand-alone EXE; the VBRUN500.DLL is required)
- Use multiple projects
- Control source code through Visual SourceSafe
- Reuse VB components
- Construct class files
- Use Data Control and data-aware controls (such as TextBox, Grid, ListBox, and ComboBox)
- Use numerous additional controls, including disk-access controls (DirListBox, DriveListBox, and so on) and user-interface controls (status bar, toolbar, and so on)

Many users do not need these extra features. For professional-level development, however, use of the full Visual Basic system is essential. Additionally, VBA applications require the Office application itself to execute. This adds to memory and hard disk space overhead for the deployed system.

VB Script in Outlook and Internet Explorer

The VB Script environment is far different from the VBA environment. VB Script programming environments are diverging as the language is included in increasingly varied applications. The dominant VB Script environment is the Outlook groupware application included with Microsoft Office.

Figure 1-4 shows the Outlook design environment when an item is placed in Design mode. The normally invisible development tabs are displayed, and controls may be inserted on the tab form. The tabs that have titles enclosed in parentheses are currently invisible

System   User modifiable
tabbed page   tabbed page

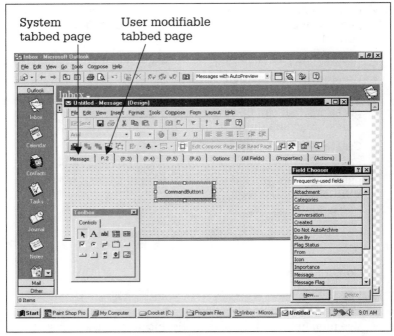

Figure 1-4.   Outlook Forms environment

to the user. You can access the VB Script environment only from the Design mode. Selecting the View Code option under the Form menu will display the Scripting window.

Changes and code written in the VB Script environment are stored with the particular form being displayed. This form can be stored to an Exchange server, where all of the code and controls will be kept with it. An Outlook user accessing the groupware server will then receive the form as well as any additions that have been made to it.

The Outlook Scripting window, shown in Figure 1-5, is an extremely rudimentary text-editing window. Code is entered into the window and may be executed as in the Immediate window by selecting the Run option from the Script menu.

Note that VB Script does not include any of the common Constant values that are so often used in VBA. VB Script can only accept the

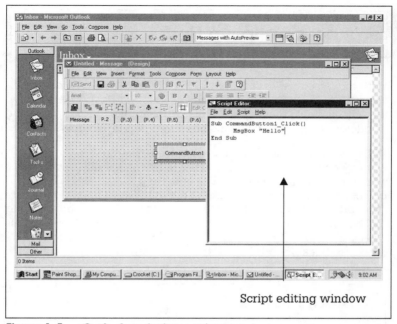

Script editing window

Figure 1-5.   Outlook scripting environment

actual values of the Constants, making it more portable. Bringing along large files of Constants would severely limit its portability.

Internet Explorer is moving through a dramatic change from version 3 to version 4. The implementation of Dynamic HTML and "scriplets" that can be used in Internet Explorer 4 will jumpstart VB Script development within web pages. Internet Explorer does not have a VB Script development environment since the code is embedded within the HTML code. However, watch for future versions of Microsoft's Visual Interdev to create a general VB Script environment.

The other VB Script environments are rapidly evolving. The newest VB Script edition, Windows Scripting Host (WSH), is merely a command line that can be used from the operating system. The user interface on WSH will most likely evolve as it becomes a full-featured tool.

Windows Scripting Host

With the introduction of Windows 98, VB Script will be included in the system itself. Known as Windows Scripting Host (WSH), it is already available for download and installation on Windows 95 and Windows NT. It will also be included as a part of Windows NT 5.0.

WSH uses the actual VB Script engine, so all of the VB Script commands denoted in this manual will be completely functional as part of the operating system. The operating system will have an object model that allows control of networks, disk operations, and other processes. Microsoft has decided not to finalize the object model for the OS until more progress has been made on Windows NT 5.0. Check the BackOffice web page (**http://www.microsoft.com/products/backoffice/**) for the latest information on this technology.

Object Browser

The Object Browser is provided as part of the Visual Basic and VBA environments. It is not included with the current version of Outlook or Internet Explorer, although their object models can be accessed through the browser.

In Figure 1-6, you'll see the Object Browser, which is available under the View menu, from an icon on the toolbar, or by pressing F2. The Object Browser contains three panes: the Classes pane, the Members pane, and the Search pane. The Libraries combo box shows what libraries are being shown in the various panes.

The *Classes* pane displays an alphabetical list of all of the available objects and collections. In Part III of this book, you will find the complete Object Model diagrams for all of the Office applications as well as other components. Using these diagrams in conjunction with the Object Browser, you can to create nearly any object-based solution. Clicking on an object or collection in the Classes pane will automatically change the members shown in the Members pane.

The *Members* pane contains all of the properties and methods for an object class (object or collection) shown in the Classes pane.

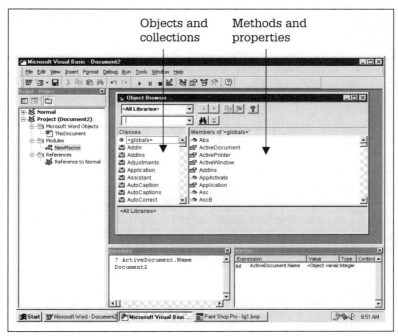

Figure 1-6.   Object Browser

Methods have an icon that looks like a speeding box. Properties have the traditional icon (the small hand pointing to the list of items) that represents properties. By clicking on a particular member, you will fill the bottom of the dialog box with its calling conventions. If the member is a property, clicking it will detail the data type held in that property. Clicking a method will show any values that it requires to be passed as arguments and any values it will return.

The *Search* pane is hidden until you activate a search. To the right of the Search button (the button with the binoculars icon), the double down-arrow icon expands the Search pane. The results of a search will appear in the pane along with the object model in which the method or property occurs.

All of the objects shown in the Object Browser are the object libraries assigned to the current project. This does not mean that these are the only libraries registered with your system. For example, Excel defaults to adding the Excel object libraries to the project, but doesn't add the Word libraries, because most people will not need them in an Excel project.

To add other libraries to the project, select the References menu option. Which menu has the References option depends on the application you are using. The References dialog box is shown in Figure 1-7. All of the boxes with checks denote the object libraries currently available to your project. By selecting others, you can add them to your project. They will automatically be added to the Libraries combo box of the Object Browser.

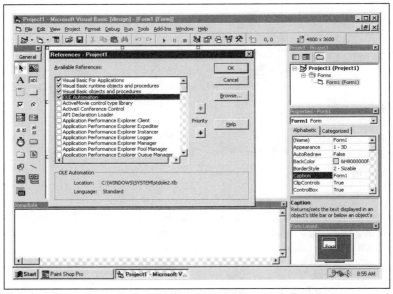

Figure 1-7. Object references available to the project

ASCII Chart

Often while working on a complex programming project, you will need to directly access characters in the format in which the computer stores them. ASCII is the standard for the relation between a number value and a character type. Each character consists of a single byte, or eight bits. Some of the characters cannot be displayed as characters, but are instead used as control characters (such as 7, the bell). In these cases the Character column is empty, but the Title column describes the character.

The following ASCII chart shows the values of all of the characters from 0 through 255. The chart includes the decimal and hexadecimal values of the characters, as well as a basic character name and title of the character. The Label column shows the traditional one- or two-letter abbreviation for 7-bit ASCII characters. The 7-bit character values were used primarily for communications when ASCII was first becoming a standard.

Additionally, the values for the characters within the newer Unicode standard is included. Unicode represents each character as two bytes (16 bits), to accommodate the numerous extra characters of various non-English alphabets.

Decimal	Char	Label	Hex	Unicode	Title
0		<NU>	/x00	<U0000>	Null (Nul)
1		<SH>	/x01	<U0001>	Start of heading (Soh)
2		<SX>	/x02	<U0002>	Start of text (Stx)
3		<EX>	/x03	<U0003>	End of text (Etx)
4		<ET>	/x04	<U0004>	End of transmission (Eot)
5		<EQ>	/x05	<U0005>	Enquiry (Enq)
6		<AK>	/x06	<U0006>	Acknowledge (Ack)
7		<BL>	/x07	<U0007>	Bell (Bel)
8		<BS>	/x08	<U0008>	Backspace (Bs)
9		<HT>	/x09	<U0009>	Character tabulation (Ht)
10		<LF>	/x0A	<U000A>	Line feed (Lf)
11		<VT>	/x0B	<U000B>	Line tabulation (Vt)
12		<FF>	/x0C	<U000C>	Form feed (Ff)
13		<CR>	/x0D	<U000D>	Carriage return (Cr)
14		<SO>	/x0E	<U000E>	Shift out (So)
15		<SI>	/x0F	<U000F>	Shift in (Si)
16		<DL>	/x10	<U0010>	Datalink escape (Dle)
17		<D1>	/x11	<U0011>	Device control one (Dc1)

Decimal	Char	Label	Hex	Unicode	Title
18		\<D2>	/x12	\<U0012>	Device control two (Dc2)
19		\<D3>	/x13	\<U0013>	Device control three (Dc3)
20		\<D4>	/x14	\<U0014>	Device control four (Dc4)
21		\<NK>	/x15	\<U0015>	Negative acknowledge (Nak)
22		\<SY>	/x16	\<U0016>	Synchronous idle (Syn)
23		\<EB>	/x17	\<U0017>	End of transmission block (Etb)
24		\<CN>	/x18	\<U0018>	Cancel (Can)
25		\<EM>	/x19	\<U0019>	End of medium (Em)
26		\<SB>	/x1A	\<U001A>	Substitute (Sub)
27		\<EC>	/x1B	\<U001B>	Escape (Esc)
28		\<FS>	/x1C	\<U001C>	File separator (Is4)
29		\<GS>	/x1D	\<U001D>	Group separator (Is3)
30		\<RS>	/x1E	\<U001E>	Record separator (Is2)
31		\<US>	/x1F	\<U001F>	Unit separator (Is1)
32		\<SP>	/x20	\<U0020>	Space
33	!	\<!>	/x21	\<U0021>	Exclamation mark
34	"	\<">	/x22	\<U0022>	Quotation mark
35	#	\<Nb>	/x23	\<U0023>	Number sign
36	$	\<DO>	/x24	\<U0024>	Dollar sign
37	%	\<%>	/x25	\<U0025>	Percent sign
38	&	\<&>	/x26	\<U0026>	Ampersand
39		\<'>	/x27	\<U0027>	Apostrophe
40	(	\<(>	/x28	\<U0028>	Left parenthesis
41	)	\<)>	/x29	\<U0029>	Right parenthesis
42	*	\<*>	/x2A	\<U002A>	Asterisk
43	+	\<+>	/x2B	\<U002B>	Plus sign
44	,	\<,>	/x2C	\<U002C>	Comma
45	-	\<->	/x2D	\<U002D>	Hyphen-minus
46	.	\<.>	/x2E	\<U002E>	Full stop
47	/	\<//>	/x2F	\<U002F>	Solidus
48	0	\<0>	/x30	\<U0030>	Digit zero
49	1	\<1>	/x31	\<U0031>	Digit one
50	2	\<2>	/x32	\<U0032>	Digit two

Decimal	Char	Label	Hex	Unicode	Title
51	3	<3>	/x33	<U0033>	Digit three
52	4	<4>	/x34	<U0034>	Digit four
53	5	<5>	/x35	<U0035>	Digit five
54	6	<6>	/x36	<U0036>	Digit six
55	7	<7>	/x37	<U0037>	Digit seven
56	8	<8>	/x38	<U0038>	Digit eight
57	9	<9>	/x39	<U0039>	Digit nine
58	:	<:>	/x3A	<U003A>	Colon
59	;	<;>	/x3B	<U003B>	Semicolon
60	<	<<>	/x3C	<U003C>	Less-than sign
61	=	<=>	/x3D	<U003D>	Equal sign
62	>	</>>	/x3E	<U003E>	Greater-than sign
63	?	<?>	/x3F	<U003F>	Question mark
64	@	<At>	/x40	<U0040>	Commercial "at"
65	A	<A>	/x41	<U0041>	Latin capital letter A
66	B	<B>	/x42	<U0042>	Latin capital letter B
67	C	<C>	/x43	<U0043>	Latin capital letter C
68	D	<D>	/x44	<U0044>	Latin capital letter D
69	E	<E>	/x45	<U0045>	Latin capital letter E
70	F	<F>	/x46	<U0046>	Latin capital letter F
71	G	<G>	/x47	<U0047>	Latin capital letter G
72	H	<H>	/x48	<U0048>	Latin capital letter H
73	I	<I>	/x49	<U0049>	Latin capital letter I
74	J	<J>	/x4A	<U004A>	Latin capital letter J
75	K	<K>	/x4B	<U004B>	Latin capital letter K
76	L	<L>	/x4C	<U004C>	Latin capital letter L
77	M	<M>	/x4D	<U004D>	Latin capital letter M
78	N	<N>	/x4E	<U004E>	Latin capital letter N
79	O	<O>	/x4F	<U004F>	Latin capital letter O
80	P	<P>	/x50	<U0050>	Latin capital letter P
81	Q	<Q>	/x51	<U0051>	Latin capital letter Q
82	R	<R>	/x52	<U0052>	Latin capital letter R
83	S	<S>	/x53	<U0053>	Latin capital letter S
84	T	<T>	/x54	<U0054>	Latin capital letter T
85	U	<U>	/x55	<U0055>	Latin capital letter U
86	V	<V>	/x56	<U0056>	Latin capital letter V
87	W	<W>	/x57	<U0057>	Latin capital letter W

Decimal	Char	Label	Hex	Unicode	Title
88	X	<X>	/x58	<U0058>	Latin capital letter X
89	Y	<Y>	/x59	<U0059>	Latin capital letter Y
90	Z	<Z>	/x5A	<U005A>	Latin capital letter Z
91	[	<<(>	/x5B	<U005B>	Left square bracket
92	\	<////>	/x5C	<U005C>	Reverse solidus
93	]	<)/>>	/x5D	<U005D>	Right square bracket
94	^	<'/>>	/x5E	<U005E>	Circumflex accent
95	_	<_>	/x5F	<U005F>	Low line
96	`	<'!>	/x60	<U0060>	Grave accent
97	a	<a>	/x61	<U0061>	Latin small letter A
98	b	<b>	/x62	<U0062>	Latin small letter B
99	c	<c>	/x63	<U0063>	Latin small letter C
100	d	<d>	/x64	<U0064>	Latin small letter D
101	e	<e>	/x65	<U0065>	Latin small letter E
102	f	<f>	/x66	<U0066>	Latin small letter F
103	g	<g>	/x67	<U0067>	Latin small letter G
104	h	<h>	/x68	<U0068>	Latin small letter H
105	i	<i>	/x69	<U0069>	Latin small letter I
106	j	<j>	/x6A	<U006A>	Latin small letter J
107	k	<k>	/x6B	<U006B>	Latin small letter K
108	l	<l>	/x6C	<U006C>	Latin small letter L
109	m	<m>	/x6D	<U006D>	Latin small letter M
110	n	<n>	/x6E	<U006E>	Latin small letter N
111	o	<o>	/x6F	<U006F>	Latin small letter O
112	p	<p>	/x70	<U0070>	Latin small letter P
113	q	<q>	/x71	<U0071>	Latin small letter Q
114	r	<r>	/x72	<U0072>	Latin small letter R
115	s	<s>	/x73	<U0073>	Latin small letter S
116	t	<t>	/x74	<U0074>	Latin small letter T
117	u	<u>	/x75	<U0075>	Latin small letter U
118	v	<v>	/x76	<U0076>	Latin small letter V
119	w	<w>	/x77	<U0077>	Latin small letter W
120	x	<x>	/x78	<U0078>	Latin small letter X
121	y	<y>	/x79	<U0079>	Latin small letter Y
122	z	<z>	/x7A	<U007A>	Latin small letter Z
123	{	<(!>	/x7B	<U007B>	Left curly bracket
124	|	<!!>	/x7C	<U007C>	Vertical line

Decimal	Char	Label	Hex	Unicode	Title
125	}	<!>	/x7D	<U007D>	Right curly bracket
126	~	<'?>	/x7E	<U007E>	Tilde
127	•	<DT>	/x7F	<U007F>	Delete (Del)
128	•		/x80	<U0080>	Extended control characters
129	•		/x81	<U0081>	Extended control characters
130	,		/x82	<U0082>	Extended control characters
131	ƒ		/x83	<U0083>	Extended control characters
132	„		/x84	<U0084>	Extended control characters
133	…		/x85	<U0085>	Extended control characters
134	†		/x86	<U0086>	Extended control characters
135	‡		/x87	<U0087>	Extended control characters
136	ˆ		/x88	<U0088>	Extended control characters
137	‰		/x89	<U0089>	Extended control characters
138	Š		/x8A	<U008A>	Extended control characters
139	‹		/x8B	<U008B>	Extended control characters
140	Œ		/x8C	<U008C>	Extended control characters
141	•		/x8D	<U008D>	Extended control characters
142	•		/x8E	<U008E>	Extended control characters
143	•		/x8F	<U008F>	Extended control characters
144	•		/x90	<U0090>	Extended control characters
145	'		/x91	<U0091>	Extended control characters

Decimal	Char	Label	Hex	Unicode	Title
146	'		/x92	<U0092>	Extended control characters
147	"		/x93	<U0093>	Extended control characters
148	"		/x94	<U0094>	Extended control characters
149	•		/x95	<U0095>	Extended control characters
150	–		/x96	<U0096>	Extended control characters
151	—		/x97	<U0097>	Extended control characters
152	˜		/x98	<U0098>	Extended control characters
153	™		/x99	<U0099>	Extended control characters
154	š		/x9A	<U009A>	Extended control characters
155	›		/x9B	<U009B>	Extended control characters
156	œ		/x9C	<U009C>	Extended control characters
157	•		/x9D	<U009D>	Extended control characters
158	•		/x9E	<U009E>	Extended control characters
159	Ÿ		/x9F	<U009F>	Extended control characters
160			/xA0	<U00A0>	Nonbreaking space
161	¡		/xA1	<U00A1>	Inverted exclamation mark
162	¢		/xA2	<U00A2>	Cent sign
163	£		/xA3	<U00A3>	Pound sterling sign
164	¤		/xA4	<U00A4>	General currency sign
165	¥		/xA5	<U00A5>	Yen sign
166	¦		/xA6	<U00A6>	Broken vertical bar
167	§		/xA7	<U00A7>	Section sign
168	¨		/xA8	<U00A8>	Spacing dieresis or umlaut

Decimal	Char	Label	Hex	Unicode	Title
169	©		/xA9	<U00A9>	Copyright sign
170	ª		/xAA	<U00AA>	Feminine ordinal indicator
171	«		/xAB	<U00AB>	Left (double) angle quote (guillemet)
172	¬		/xAC	<U00AC>	Logical "not" sign
173	-		/xAD	<U00AD>	Soft hyphen
174	®		/xAE	<U00AE>	Registered trademark sign
175	‾		/xAF	<U00AF>	Spacing macron (long) accent
176	°		/xB0	<U00B0>	Degree sign
177	±		/xB1	<U00B1>	Plus-or-minus sign
178	²		/xB2	<U00B2>	Superscript 2
179	³		/xB3	<U00B3>	Superscript 3
180	´		/xB4	<U00B4>	Spacing acute accent
181	µ		/xB5	<U00B5>	Micro sign
182	¶		/xB6	<U00B6>	Paragraph sign, pilcrow sign
183	·		/xB7	<U00B7>	Middle dot, centered dot
184	¸		/xB8	<U00B8>	Spacing cedilla
185	¹		/xB9	<U00B9>	Superscript 1
186	º		/xBA	<U00BA>	Masculine ordinal indicator
187	»		/xBB	<U00BB>	Right (double) angle quote (guillemet)
188	¼		/xBC	<U00BC>	Fraction 1/4
189	½		/xBD	<U00BD>	Fraction 1/2
190	¾		/xBE	<U00BE>	Fraction 3/4
191	¿		/xBF	<U00BF>	Inverted question mark
192	À		/xC0	<U00C0>	Capital A grave
193	Á		/xC1	<U00C1>	Capital A acute
194	Â		/xC2	<U00C2>	Capital A circumflex
195	Ã		/xC3	<U00C3>	Capital A tilde
196	Ä		/xC4	<U00C4>	Capital A dieresis or umlaut

Decimal	Char	Label	Hex	Unicode	Title
197	Å		/xC5	<U00C5>	Capital A ring
198	Æ		/xC6	<U00C6>	Capital AE ligature
199	Ç		/xC7	<U00C7>	Capital C cedilla
200	È		/xC8	<U00C8>	Capital E grave
201	É		/xC9	<U00C9>	Capital E acute
202	Ê		/xCA	<U00CA>	Capital E circumflex
203	Ë		/xCB	<U00CB>	Capital E dieresis or umlaut
204	Ì		/xCC	<U00CC>	Capital I grave
205	Í		/xCD	<U00CD>	Capital I acute
206	Î		/xCE	<U00CE>	Capital I circumflex
207	Ï		/xCF	<U00CF>	Capital I dieresis or umlaut
208	Ð		/xD0	<U00D0>	Capital eth
209	Ñ		/xD1	<U00D1>	Capital N tilde
210	Ò		/xD2	<U00D2>	Capital O grave
211	Ó		/xD3	<U00D3>	Capital O acute
212	Ô		/xD4	<U00D4>	Capital O circumflex
213	Õ		/xD5	<U00D5>	Capital O tilde
214	Ö		/xD6	<U00D6>	Capital O dieresis or umlaut
215	×		/xD7	<U00D7>	Multiplication sign
216	Ø		/xD8	<U00D8>	Capital O slash
217	Ù		/xD9	<U00D9>	Capital U grave
218	Ú		/xDA	<U00DA>	Capital U acute
219	Û		/xDB	<U00DB>	Capital U circumflex
220	Ü		/xDC	<U00DC>	Capital U dieresis or umlaut
221	Ý		/xDD	<U00DD>	Capital Y acute
222	Þ		/xDE	<U00DE>	Capital thorn
223	ß		/xDF	<U00DF>	Small sharp S, SZ ligature
224	à		/xE0	<U00E0>	Small A grave
225	á		/xE1	<U00E1>	Small A acute
226	â		/xE2	<U00E2>	Small A circumflex
227	ã		/xE3	<U00E3>	Small A tilde
228	ä		/xE4	<U00E4>	Small A dieresis or umlaut

Decimal	Char	Label	Hex	Unicode	Title
229	å		/xE5	<U00E5>	Small A ring
230	æ		/xE6	<U00E6>	Small AE ligature
231	ç		/xE7	<U00E7>	Small C cedilla
232	è		/xE8	<U00E8>	Small E grave
233	é		/xE9	<U00E9>	Small E acute
234	ê		/xEA	<U00EA>	Small E circumflex
235	ë		/xEB	<U00EB>	Small E dieresis or umlaut
236	ì		/xEC	<U00EC>	Small I grave
237	í		/xED	<U00ED>	Small I acute
238	î		/xEE	<U00EE>	Small I circumflex
239	ï		/xEF	<U00EF>	Small I dieresis or umlaut
240	ð		/xF0	<U00F0>	Small eth
241	ñ		/xF1	<U00F1>	Small N tilde
242	ò		/xF2	<U00F2>	Small O grave
243	ó		/xF3	<U00F3>	Small O acute
244	ô		/xF4	<U00F4>	Small O circumflex
245	õ		/xF5	<U00F5>	Small O tilde
246	ö		/xF6	<U00F6>	Small O dieresis or umlaut
247	÷		/xF7	<U00F7>	Division sign
248	ø		/xF8	<U00F8>	Small O slash
249	ù		/xF9	<U00F9>	Small U grave
250	ú		/xFA	<U00FA>	Small U acute
251	û		/xFB	<U00FB>	Small U circumflex
252	ü		/xFC	<U00FC>	Small U dieresis or umlaut
253	ý		/xFD	<U00FD>	Small Y acute
254	þ		/xFE	<U00FE>	Small thorn
255	ÿ		/xFF	<U00FF>	Small Y dieresis or umlaut

Error Chart

Visual Basic allows you to identify through a trap most of the errors that occur with your program. By writing a comprehensive debugging routine or using a product such as VB/Rig to create error-checking routines, you will save your users a great deal of time and save yourself debugging efforts. Technical support calls are very difficult to handle without a clear understanding of which problem actually occurred.

The following chart provides a list of all the trappable errors and the descriptions that will be returned by the Error$( ) function. You can use the Error$( ) function yourself within your program to provide an English description of the error that occurs.

Error Number	Description
3	Return without GoSub
5	Invalid procedure call or argument
6	Overflow
7	Out of memory
9	Subscript out of range
10	This array is fixed or temporarily locked
11	Division by zero
13	Type mismatch
14	Out of string space
16	Expression too complex
17	Can't perform requested operation
18	User interrupt occurred
20	Resume without error
28	Out of stack space
35	Sub or Function not defined
47	Too many DLL application clients
48	Error in loading DLL
49	Bad DLL calling convention
51	Internal error
52	Bad file name or number
53	File not found
54	Bad file mode

Error Number	Description
55	File already open
57	Device I/O error
58	File already exists
59	Bad record length
61	Disk full
62	Input past end of file
63	Bad record number
67	Too many files
68	Device unavailable
70	Permission denied
71	Disk not ready
74	Can't rename with different drive
75	Path/File access error
76	Path not found
91	Object variable or With block variable not set
92	For loop not initialized
93	Invalid pattern string
94	Invalid use of Null
96	Unable to sink events of object because the object is already firing events to the maximum number of event receivers that it supports
97	Cannot call friend function on object which is not an instance of defining class
321	Invalid file format
322	Can't create necessary temporary file
325	Invalid format in resource file
380	Invalid property value
381	Invalid property array index
382	Set not supported at runtime
383	Set not supported (read-only property)
385	Need property array index
387	Set not permitted
393	Get not supported at runtime
394	Get not supported (write-only property)
422	Property not found
423	Property or method not found
424	Object required

Error Number	Description
429	ActiveX component can't create object
430	Class doesn't support Automation
432	File name or class name not found during Automation operation
438	Object doesn't support this property or method
440	Automation error
442	Connection to type library or object library for remote process has been lost. Press OK for dialog to remove reference
443	Automation object does not have a default value
445	Object doesn't support this action
446	Object doesn't support named arguments
447	Object doesn't support current locale setting
448	Named argument not found
449	Argument not optional
450	Wrong number of arguments or invalid property assignment
451	Object not a collection
452	Invalid ordinal
453	Specified DLL function not found
454	Code resource not found
455	Code resource lock error
457	This key is already associated with an element of this collection
458	Variable uses an Automation type not supported in Visual Basic
459	Object or class does not support the set of events
460	Invalid clipboard format
481	Invalid picture
482	Printer error
735	Can't save file to TEMP
744	Search text not found
746	Replacements too long
31001	Out of memory
31004	No object
31018	Class is not set
31027	Unable to activate object

Error Number	Description
31032	Unable to create embedded object
31036	Error saving to file
31037	Error loading from file

Command Groups

Finding the correct command or group of commands to accomplish a particular task is often very difficult. To aid you in finding the functions that you need, here is a reference that groups commands into the following areas: Financial, Mathematical, Disk Access, Date and Time, Strings, and Display. Each table contains all of the Visual Basic commands that relate to the specific area. In Part II, after you have located one of the commands you need, the "See Also" references included with each command will also guide you to similar commands.

Financial

Here are the Visual Basic financial commands:

DDB	CCur	MIRR	PMT	Rate
DefCur	IPmt	NPer	PPmt	SLN
FV	IRR	NPV	PV	SYD

Disk Access

These are the Visual Basic disk-access commands:

ChDir	FileCopy	InputB, inputB$
ChDrive	FileDateTime	Kill
Close	FileLen	Line Input #
CurDir, CurDir$	FreeFile	Loc
Dir, Dir$	Get	Lock...Unlock
Environ, Environ$	GetAttr	LOF
EOF	Input #	MkDir
FileAttr	Input, input$	Name

Open	RmDir	Spc
Print #	Seek	Width #
Put	SetAttr	Write #
Reset		

Mathematical

Here are Visual Basic's mathematical commands:

*	\	DefDbl	Imp	Rnd
+	^	DefInt	Int	Sgn
-	And	DefLng	IsNumeric	Sin
/	CDbl	DefSng	Log	Sqr
<=	CDec	Eqv	Mod	Tan
<>	CInt	Exp	Not	TRUE
=	CLng	FALSE	Oct,Oct$	Xor
>	Cos	Fix	Or	
>=	CSng	Hex, Hex$	Randomize	

Date and Time

These are the Visual Basic commands related to date and time:

CVDate	DateSerial	Month	TimeSerial
Date	DateValue	Now	TimeValue
Date, Date$	Day	Second	WeekDay
DateAdd	Hour	Time	Year
DateDiff	IsDate	Time$	
DatePart	Minute	Timer	

Strings

These are the Visual Basic commands pertaining to strings:

&	ChrB	DefStr
+	ChrW	Format, Format$
Chr, Chr$	CStr	Instr

LCase, Lcase$	Option Compare	String, String$
Left, Left$	Right,Right$	Tab
Len	RSet	Trim, Trim$
LenB	RTrim,RTrim$	Ucase, UCase$
Lset	Space,Space$	Val
LTrim, LTrim$	Str, Str$	
Mid, Mid$	StrComp	

Display

Here are Visual Basic's display commands:

Circle	Line	QBColor
Cls	PaintPicture	Pset
Draw	Print	RGB

VB Script Missing Commands

VB Script is a subset of the entire Visual Basic instruction set. Most of the key Visual Basic commands are included in VB Script. Excluded are all disk-access and financial functions. These commands were removed for security and space reasons. The entire VB Script language DLL requires less than 10 percent of the disk space of the VBA 5 run time.

As VB Script grows in popularity and becomes incorporated into the Windows operating system with the release of Windows 98 and Windows NT 5, understanding the functions that are missing will be increasingly important before you begin a new programming project. Then you can plan around missing capabilities. Most of the missing functionality can be created either by combining existing commands or by using a supplemental object that supplies the missing operation.

Active Server Pages, Microsoft's dynamic web server component, uses objects in exactly this way to extend the VB Script included. A disk access object, for example, provides complete file features. In this manner, each VB Script environment can include the necessary custom features without having to rewrite or directly extend the language.

!	FreeFile	PPmt
#Const	FV	Print #
#if...#else...#endif	Get	Property Get
ChDir	GetAttr	Property Let
ChDrive	GoSub...Return	Property Set
Close	GoTo	Put
CurDir, CurDir$	Input #	PV
CVar	Input, input$	Rate
CVDate	InputB, inputB$	Reset
Date, Date$	Ipmt	Resume
DDB	IRR	RmDir
Declare	Kill	Rollback
DefBool	Like	RSet
DefByte	Line Input #	SavePicture
DefCur	LoadPicture	Seek
DefDbl	Loc	SetAttr
DefInt	Lock...Unlock	SLN
DefLng	LOF	Spc
DefObj	LSet	Static
DefSng	Mid, Mid$	Stop
DefStr	MIRR	Str, Str$
DefVar	MkDir	SYD
Dir, Dir$	Name	Time
DoEvents	NPer	Time$
End	NPV	Timer
EOF	On Error...	Type...End Type
Err object	On...GoSub	Val
Error	On...GoTo	Width #
FileAttr	Open	With...End With
FileCopy	Option Base	Write #
FileDateTime	Option Compare	
FileLen	PMT	

Part II
Language Reference

> **!**

Database field operator

Description
Using the exclamation command (!) allows you to access a database field while bypassing a complete database field object reference. The Immediate window example requires a RecordSet created with the name "myRS" and containing a field titled "LastName."

AVAILABLE IN VB SCRIPT

Syntax
```
recordset!field
```

Parameters
recordset   Required. Recordset of dynaset, table, or snapshot type.

field   Required. Field contained in the recordset.

Returns
N/A

Immediate Window Sample
```
? myRS!LastName
```

User Tip
The exclamation command can be used to quickly reference fields in a database instead of using a complete Fields("LastName") reference.

SEE ALSO   Fields, &

Double operator

Description
This operator will set the variable to be a Double type.

AVAILABLE IN VB SCRIPT

Syntax
a#

Parameters
a Any permitted variable name

Returns
N/A

Immediate Window Sample
a# = 56

SEE ALSO CDbl, DefDbl

#

Used to enclose a Date type

Description
Surrounding a date or time value with the # sign will generate the proper Date value.

AVAILABLE IN VB SCRIPT

Syntax
#date#

Parameters

date   Required. Any valid date or time.

Returns

Variant type

Immediate Window Sample

```
? #1/2/97#
```

SEE ALSO   CVDate

#Const

Conditional compile constant

Description

This operator creates a private constant in a module. The conditional compiler treats these constants as literals. Therefore, when the program is actually compiled, there is no speed difference from using the actual value.

NOT AVAILABLE IN VB SCRIPT

Syntax

```
#Const constname = expression
```

Parameters

constname   Any permitted variable name.

Expression   Can include an operator (except Is) or a numeric value.

Returns

N/A

Immediate Window Sample

N/A

SEE ALSO   #if...#else...#endif, Const

#if...#else...#endif

Conditional compilation of a section of code

Description

Using the conditional compile adds the code encapsulated only if
the condition is true. This can be used to include or exclude demo
code or, in Visual Basic 4.0, to provide conditional code for a 16- or
32-bit compile. It also can check for execution on the Macintosh for
special Macintosh-related code. Compile time variables include
Mac and Win32 to determine the type of execution system.

AVAILABLE IN VB SCRIPT

Syntax

```
#if condition-1 Then " [actions-1] : [#ElseIf
condition-2 Then] : [actions-2] : [#Elself
condition-n Then] : [actions-n] : [#Else] : [else-
actions] : #End If
```

Parameters

conditions   Required. Boolean expressions.

Returns

N/A

Immediate Window Sample

N/A

SEE ALSO   #Const

$

Sets the type of the variable to a string

Description

This string operator serves the same function as defining a variable
with the 'Dim x As String' command. Once the operator is used in a

definition, the variable name without the operator can be used to access the same variable (that is, myString$ and myString address the same variable).

AVAILABLE IN VB SCRIPT

Syntax
```
a$
```

Parameters
a   Any permitted variable name

Returns
N/A

Immediate Window Sample
```
a$ = "Hello" & 2
? a$
? a
```

SEE ALSO   CStr, Dim, DefStr

Sets the type of the variable to an integer

Description
This string operator serves the same function as defining a variable with the 'Dim x As Integer' command. Once the operator is used in a definition, the variable name without the operator accesses the same variable.

AVAILABLE IN VB SCRIPT

Syntax
```
a%
```

Parameters
a   Any permitted variable name

Returns
N/A

Immediate Window Sample
```
a% = 5.14
? a%
? a
```

SEE ALSO   Cint, DefInt

&

String combining or concatenation operator

Description
This operator is extremely powerful because it automatically converts between types as it combines or concatenates into a resultant string. Therefore, it can be used to combine several different variable types into a string without any explicit conversion.

AVAILABLE IN VB SCRIPT

Syntax
```
a & b
```

Parameters
a, b   Any variant or data types

Returns
Variant

Immediate Window Sample
```
? "a" & 12 & 1.22 & #1/2/97#
```

User Tip
The & operator can prevent database errors when you're dealing with Nulls. If you set a string to a field that contains a Null, as in myStr$=myRS!myField, an error will occur. To prevent the error, use myStr$="" & myRS!myField.

SEE ALSO   +, !, cstr

'

Remark command

Description

The apostrophe (') command can be used to mark code as a remark
to be ignored by the compiler. In the Immediate window, Visual
Basic will also ignore any command that follows it.

AVAILABLE IN VB SCRIPT

Syntax

```
' comment
```

Parameters

comment   Any text

Returns

N/A

Immediate Window Sample

```
' ? "1"
```

User Tip

During development, when a line of code isn't needed anymore,
make the line a comment rather than deleting it. Therefore, if
conditions change before the project completes and the code is
needed, the comment can be removed rather than rewriting the
code.

SEE ALSO   Rem

*

Multiplication operator

Description

The multiplication operator will multiply one number by another and provide the result.

AVAILABLE IN VB SCRIPT

Syntax

```
a * b
```

Parameters

a, b   Required. Any valid numeric expression.

Returns

Variant

Immediate Window Sample

```
? 2.12 * 3.14
```

SEE ALSO   ∧, /, +, -, Mod, \

Addition operator

Description

This operator adds one number to another and provides the result.

AVAILABLE IN VB SCRIPT

Syntax

```
a + b
```

Parameters

a, b   Required. Any valid numeric expression.

Returns

Variant

Immediate Window Sample
```
? 2.12 + 3.14
```

SEE ALSO   ∧, /, *, -, Mod, \

String addition operator

Description
The + operator can be used many times within a single line to create a large combination of strings. Unlike using the & operator, if you try to create a string using the + operator with multiple variable types, a "Type Mismatch" error will occur. Use the & operator to avoid the error.

AVAILABLE IN VB SCRIPT

Syntax
```
a + b
```

Parameters
a, b   Required. Any valid expression.

Returns
Variant

Immediate Window Sample
```
? "U.S. economy..." + "Status: " + "ok."
```

SEE ALSO   &, cstr

Subtraction or negation operator

Description

This operator will subtract one number from another and provide the result.

AVAILABLE IN VB SCRIPT

Syntax

```
a - b
```

Parameters

a, b Required. Any valid numeric expression.

Returns

Variant

Immediate Window Sample

```
? -1
? 5 - 3
? 3 - 5
```

SEE ALSO ∧, /, *, +, Mod, \

/

Division operator

Description

This operator divides one number by another and provides the result. The result of the division will be returned in the data type appropriate to the result (i.e., 10 / 3 will be returned as a Single). Use the \ operator to force the return of an integer. Use the Mod operator to return the remainder that results in an integer division.

AVAILABLE IN VB SCRIPT

Syntax

```
a / b
```

Parameters

a, b Required. Any valid numeric expression.

Returns
Variant

Immediate Window Sample
```
? 9/3
? 9/2
```

SEE ALSO ∧, +, *, -, Mod, \

Less-than operator

Description
Using the Less-than operator can compare two numeric values and returns the Boolean True or False depending on the result. If you send this operator values such as strings, they will be evaluated by their alphabetical values, including case sensitivity. Some of the Immediate window operators demonstrate the nonintuitive results.

AVAILABLE IN VB SCRIPT

Syntax
```
a < b
```

Parameters
a, b   Required. Any valid numeric expression.

Returns
Variant

Immediate Window Sample
```
? 3 < 5
? 3 < 2
? "a" < "z"
? "z" < "a"
? "A" < "a"
? "21" < "200"
```

SEE ALSO   >, =, <>, >=, <=, Like, Not, And

Less-than or equal-to operator

Description
This operator compares two values for less-than or equivalent condition.

AVAILABLE IN VB SCRIPT

Syntax
a <= b

Parameters
a, **b**   Required. Any valid numeric expression.

Returns
Variant

Immediate Window Sample
? 1 <= 2
? 2 <= 1

SEE ALSO   =, <>, <, >, >=, Like, Not, And

Nonequality operator

Description
This operator compares two values for nonequivalent condition.

AVAILABLE IN VB SCRIPT

Syntax
a <> b

Parameters

a, b   Required. Any valid numeric expression.

Returns

Variant

Immediate Window Sample

```
? 1 <> 2
? 1 <> 1
```

SEE ALSO   =, >, <, >=, <=, Like, Not, And

Equality operator

Description

This operator compares two values for equivalent condition.

AVAILABLE IN VB SCRIPT

Syntax

```
a = b
```

Parameters

a, b   Required. Any valid numeric expression.

Returns

Variant

Immediate Window Sample

```
? 1 = 1
? 2 = 1
? True = False
```

SEE ALSO   <>, >, <, >=, <=, Like, Not, And

> **>**

Greater-than operator

Description
This operator compares two values for the greater-than condition.

AVAILABLE IN VB SCRIPT

Syntax
```
a > b
```

Parameters
a, b   Required. Any valid numeric expression.

Returns
Variant

Immediate Window Sample
```
? 5 > 3
? 3 > 5
```

SEE ALSO   =, <>, <, >=, <=, Like, Not, And

> **>=**

Greater-than or equal-to operator

Description
Use to compare two values for greater-than or equivalent condition.

AVAILABLE IN VB SCRIPT

Syntax
```
a >= b
```

Parameters

a, b   Required. Any valid numeric expression.

Returns

Variant type

Immediate Window Sample

```
? 2 >= 1
? 2 >= 2
? 1 >= 2
```

SEE ALSO   =, <>, >, <, <=, Like, Not, And

?

Prints to the current or Immediate window

Description

For quick typing, the question mark can be used in place of the Print command.

AVAILABLE IN VB SCRIPT

Syntax

```
? a
```

Parameters

a   Any valid expression

Returns

N/A

Immediate Window Sample

```
? "Hello"
```

SEE ALSO   Print, Space, Space$, Tab

Integer division operator

Description

This performs like the traditional division (/) operator, except it returns the results as an integer. Before the division takes place, both numbers are converted to integers. The result is truncated rather than rounded to the nearest integer. Use the Mod operator to obtain the remainder of the division of two integers.

AVAILABLE IN VB SCRIPT

Syntax

a \ b

Parameters

a, b   Required. Any valid numeric expression.

Returns

Variant type

Immediate Window Sample

```
? 16 \ 8
? 16 \ 15
```

SEE ALSO   ^, +, *, -, Mod, /

Exponent or caret operator

Description

This returns the number raised to the power of the provided exponent.

AVAILABLE IN VB SCRIPT

Syntax
```
a ^ b
```

Parameters
a, b   Required. Any valid numeric expression.

Returns
Variant

Immediate Window Sample
```
? 2 ^ 1
? 2 ^ 2
? 2 ^ 8
? 2 ^ 0
```

SEE ALSO   +, *, -, Mod, \, /

And

Logical And

Description
This command can be used to compile two comparison expressions or to logically combine two numbers. The And operator will return the bitwise result of all bits that exist in both values.

AVAILABLE IN VB SCRIPT

Syntax
```
a And b
```

Parameters
a, b   Required. Any valid numeric expression.

Returns
Variant

Immediate Window Sample
```
? (2 > 1) and (2 > 0)
? (2 > 3) and (2 > 0)
? 15 and 8
? 16 and 8
? 256 and 8
```

SEE ALSO   Or, Imp, Eqv, Xor, True, False

AppActivate

Activates a specified application window

Description
This command will shift the focus to any application currently running under the Windows system. Either the title of the window or the application ID that is returned by the Shell command may be used. Note that activating the application does not change the collapsed or expanded state of the application.

AVAILABLE IN VB SCRIPT

Syntax
```
AppActivate title[, wait]
```

Parameters
title   Required.

wait   Optional.

Returns
N/A

Immediate Window Sample
```
AppActivate "Microsoft Excel"
MyAppID = Shell("C:\Office\WINWORD.EXE", 1)
AppActivate MyAppID
```

User Tip

To avoid multiple instances of a single application executing, this command can be used. If an instance is already running, the new instance simply activates the existent application and shuts itself down.

SEE ALSO   Shell, Environ$

Beep

Speaker beep

Description

The Beep command will simply beep the speaker. There is no other way to make sound with Visual Basic without using the Windows API routines or the Multimedia control. Use the Windows API (see Declare statement) to play digitized sound (WAV files) or MIDI (MID files) sounds.

AVAILABLE IN VB SCRIPT

Syntax

```
Beep
```

Parameters

N/A

Returns

N/A

Immediate Window Sample

```
Beep
```

User Tip

The Beep command is excellent to place strategically in your code for debugging. By counting the number of beeps, you can determine what points of the program have executed before a problem occurred.

SEE ALSO   ?, Print, Declare

Call

Activates a procedure

Description
This executes a system or user-defined procedure. To call a subroutine, you can simply use the name of the procedure or precede the name with the Call statement to make the call more explicit in the code.

AVAILABLE IN VB SCRIPT

Syntax
```
Call name [argmentlist]
```

Parameters
name   Required. Current procedure name.

argmentlist   Optional. Any parameters required for the procedure.

Returns
N/A

Immediate Window Sample
```
Call Beep
Call MsgBox("Hello")
```

User Tip
Although a procedure can be executed by simply typing its name, the Call command allows the use of parentheses around arguments (like a function) and makes calls to outside routines more apparent in your source code.

SEE ALSO   Function, Sub

CByte

Converts to Byte data type

Description

A Byte data type takes up a single byte in the computer memory and has a value from 0 to 255. This data type is used mostly for file formats and data conversion. Converting a number greater than 255 or less than 0 results in an Overflow error.

AVAILABLE IN VB SCRIPT

Syntax

```
CByte(expression)
```

Parameters

expression   Required. Value to be converted.

Returns

Byte type

Immediate Window Sample

```
? CByte(3)
? CByte(3.2)
```

SEE ALSO   CDbl, CInt, CLng, CSng, CStr, Cvar, DefByte

CCur

Converts the variable passed to the function to a Currency type variable

Description

This conversion function can be used to ensure the type of a particular variable. It is especially useful for converting variant types to a specific variable type, which makes many routines up to four times faster.

AVAILABLE IN VB SCRIPT

Syntax

```
CCur (expression)
```

Parameters

expression   variant, integer, single, double, string

Returns

Currency type

Immediate Window Sample

```
? CCur("10.5389")
```

SEE ALSO   CDbl, CInt, CLng, CSng, CStr, Cvar, DefCur

CDbl

Converts to double floating-point number

Description

The Double type can hold from $-1.79769313486232E208$ to
$-4.94065645841247E-324$ for negative numbers or from
$4.94065645841247E-324$ to $1.79769313486232E208$ for positive
numbers.

AVAILABLE IN VB SCRIPT

Syntax

```
CDbl(expression)
```

Parameters

expression   Required. Value to be converted.

Returns

Double type

Immediate Window Sample

```
myVar = 1
mDVar = CDbl(myVar)
myDVar = myDVar / 3
? myDVar
```

User Tip

Double precision takes longer to calculate than the Single type.
Therefore, use Single if you do not need the extra accuracy.

SEE ALSO   CCur, DInt, CLng, CSng, CStr, Cvar, DefDbl

CDec

Converts to variable type Decimal

Description

The Decimal type contains numbers scaled to the power of ten. In
the background, it optimizes for numbers that do or don't contain
decimals. Without any decimals, the range is positive and negative
79,228,162,514,264,337,593,543,950,335. Numbers with decimal
places have 28 decimal places between positive and negative
7.9228162514264337593543950335.

AVAILABLE IN VB SCRIPT

Syntax

CDec(expression)

Parameters

expression   Required. Value to be converted.

Returns

Variant

Immediate Window Sample

```
? CDec(100)
? CDec(-5.231)
```

User Tip

Currently you cannot specify a type with the As operator a
Decimal. Use the CDec command to store a decimal in a variant
variable.

SEE ALSO   CDbl, CInt, CLng, CSng, CStr, Cvar, DefDec

ChDir

Changes the default directory

Description
Use the change directory (ChDir) command to change the default directory location where Visual Basic searches for files without a fully qualified path. After using this command, any open or file reference operations will access this specified folder first.

NOT AVAILABLE IN VB SCRIPT

Syntax
ChDir path$

Parameters
path$ Required. Any valid path.

Returns
N/A

Immediate Window Sample
ChDir("C:\")

SEE ALSO   ChDrive, CurDir, CurDir$, MkDir, RmDir, Open #, Dir$, Environ, Kill, MkDir, RmDir

ChDrive

Changes the currently default selected drive

Description
This command will change the current drive. This changes the default drive to the value passed in a string. If a multicharacter string is passed, only the first character is used.

NOT AVAILABLE IN VB SCRIPT

Syntax
```
ChDrive Drive$
```

Parameters
drive$ Required. String that contains a valid drive.

Returns
N/A

Immediate Window Sample
```
ChDrive "c:"
ChDrive "alpha:"
```

SEE ALSO   ChDir, CurDir, CurDir$, MkDir, RmDir, Open #, Dir$, Environ, Kill

Choose

Returns a specified value for a list

Description
This function returns a value from a list of arguments based on an index number. Can be used to quickly return a selection without having to create an array.

AVAILABLE IN VB SCRIPT

Syntax
```
Choose(index%,expression1[,expression2]...[expres-
sion13])
```

Parameters
index   Required. Number of expression to be returned.

expression   Required. Any valid expression.

Returns
Variant

Immediate Window Sample
```
? Choose(3,"Draw","Paint","Write","Build")
```

SEE ALSO   IIf, Switch, Select...Case

Chr, Chr$

Returns the character string of the ASCII value passed to it

Description
This function can be used to return both normal and unprintable characters. Common characters such as a space (Chr(32)), a tab (Chr(9)), a carriage return (Chr(13)), or a linefeed (Chr(10)) can be added to a string.

AVAILABLE IN VB SCRIPT

Syntax
```
Chr$(AsciiCode%)
Chr(AsciiCode%)
```

Parameters
AsciiCode   Required. An integer or long that defines the character.

Returns
String type

Immediate Window Sample
```
? chr(86) + chr(66) + chr(65)
```

User Tip
See the ASCII chart included in Part I of the book for a list of values.

SEE ALSO   Asc, ChrB, ChrW

ChrB

2

Converts to character string of type Byte

Description
This returns a single byte of a string. This byte conforms with the ASCII standard for files, as opposed to the newer Unicode standard, which uses two bytes per character to handle all of the international character sets.

AVAILABLE IN VB SCRIPT

Syntax
ChrB$(AsciiCode%)
ChrB(AsciiCode%)

Parameters
AsciiCode   An integer or long that defines the character

Returns
Byte type

Immediate Window Sample
? ChrB(65)

SEE ALSO   Chr, ChrW, Asc

ChrW

Converts to character type Unicode

Description
This returns a string of the character code. This string conforms with the Unicode standard, which uses two bytes per character to handle all of the international character sets.

AVAILABLE IN VB SCRIPT

Syntax

```
ChrW$(AsciiCode%)
ChrW(AsciiCode%)
```

Parameters

AsciiCode   An integer or long that defines the character

Returns

String type

Immediate Window Sample

```
? ChrW(65)
```

SEE ALSO   Chr, ChrB, Asc

CInt

Converts the given expression to an integer

Description

This converts the expression to an Integer data type. A fractional part rounds to the nearest even number. The number 1.5 will round to 2, but 2.5 will round to 2 also. Integers can range from –32,768 to 32,767.

AVAILABLE IN VB SCRIPT

Syntax

```
CInt(expression)
```

Parameters

expression   Required. Value to be converted.

Returns

Integer type

Immediate Window Sample

```
? CInt(1.25)
```

User Tip

For your loops, make sure that you explicitly define the counter variables as Integer or Long numbers (that is, Dim myVar as Integer). This can make the loop up to four times faster than variables that are left as Variant variable types.

SEE ALSO CCur, CDbl, CLng, CSng, CStr, CVar, Fix, Int, DefInt, \

CLng

Converts the given expression to a Long integer

Description

This converts the expression to an Long data type. A fractional part rounds to the nearest even number. The number 1.5 will round to 2, but 2.5 will round to 2 also.

AVAILABLE IN VB SCRIPT

Syntax

CLng(expression)

Parameters

expression Required. Value to be converted.

Returns

Long type

Immediate Window Sample

? CLng(200000.5)

SEE ALSO CCur, CDbl, CInt, CSng, CStr, CVar, Fix, Int, DefLng

Close

Closes all open files or the file specified by the file number

Description

If you omit the file number and issue the Close command, all open files will be closed.

NOT AVAILABLE IN VB SCRIPT

Syntax

```
Close [#][filenumber%][, [#]filenumber%]
```

Parameters

filenumber%   Required. Current file number to open.

Returns

N/A

Immediate Window Sample

```
Open "c:\vbtest.txt" for output as #1 :_
Print #1, "Hello World!" : Close #1
```

SEE ALSO   Open, Reset, Print #, Input

Command

Returns the commands passed to the Visual Basic program when it is executed

Description

This command is useful if you will have a file extension associated with your program. When the user double-clicks the document, your EXE is launched and the path and name of the document that was selected is passed in this string. If no commands were passed when the program was executed, this command will return an empty string.

AVAILABLE IN VB SCRIPT

Syntax

```
Command$ Command
```

Parameters
N/A

Returns
String type

Immediate Window Sample
? Command

User Tip
Use this function to retrieve commands sent to the program at the DOS prompt, such as switches and so on.

SEE ALSO   Environ, Environ$

CommitTrans

Writes transactions to database

Description
This writes all currently queued transactions into the database since the BeginTrans command was activated. Committing the transactions will write them to the database, while the Rollback command will do the opposite by aborting all transactions.

NOT AVAILABLE IN VB SCRIPT

Syntax
CommitTrans

Parameters
N/A

Returns
N/A

Immediate Window Sample
N/A

SEE ALSO   BeginTrans, Rollback

Const

Declares a value as a Constant

Description
Like the Dim command, the Const command cannot be used in the
Immediate window. Defining a Const creates a read-only variable,
in contrast to the #Const command, which actually substitutes a
value at compile time. Note that the #Const command cannot be
used in VB Script.

AVAILABLE IN VB SCRIPT

Syntax
```
[Global] Const name = expression [,name = expression]
```

Parameters
name   Required. Any permitted variable name.

expression   Required. Any valid expression.

Returns
N/A

Immediate Window Sample
N/A

SEE ALSO   DefCur, DefDbl, DefInt, DefLng, DefSng, DefStr,
DefVar, Dim, Global, ReDim, Static, #Const

Cos

Returns the cosine of an angle specified in radians

Description
This command requires the angle to be passed in radians. The
formula radians = (degrees*pi)/180 can be used to determine the
radians from a degree measure.

AVAILABLE IN VB SCRIPT

Syntax
```
Cos(angle)
```

Parameters
angle   Required. Any numeric expression holding a radian measure.

Returns
Double type

Immediate Window Sample
```
? cos(3.14159)
? cos((90*3.14159)/180)
```

SEE ALSO   Atn, Sin, Tan, Log, Exp, Sgn, Sqr

CreateObject

Creates an instance of an object

Description
Use this function to create a new instance of any OLE or ActiveX object. Either the qualified pathname (i.e. "excel.application") or the entire ClassID can be used to select the class library used to create the object.

AVAILABLE IN VB SCRIPT

Syntax
```
CreateObject(Class$)
```

Parameters
Class$ Required. Class name of the required object. Must be registered with the OLE Registry system.

Returns
Object reference

Immediate Window Sample

```
set myObject = CreateObject("excel.application")
myObject.Visible = true
```

User Tip

Make sure that any objects you create are also eliminated by using the Set myObject = Nothing command. Garbage collection routines should eliminate instances when they go out of scope, but it is good programming practice to destroy the objects explicitly.

SEE ALSO   GetObject, Set, dot (.), Nothing

CSng

Converts the given expression to a single precision floating-point number

Description

This converts to a Single data type that can hold negative numbers between −3.402823E38 and −1.401298E−45 or positive numbers between 1.401298E−45 and 3.402823E38.

AVAILABLE IN VB SCRIPT

Syntax

CSng(expression)

Parameters

expression   Required. Value to be converted.

Returns

Single type

Immediate Window Sample

? CSng(1.222)

SEE ALSO   CCur, CDbl, CInt, CLng, CStr, Cvar, DefSng

2

CStr

Converts the given expression to a string

Description
This command can be used to convert any data type to a string. Most useful are the numeric- and date-to-string conversions.

AVAILABLE IN VB SCRIPT

Syntax
CStr(expression)

Parameters
expression   Required. Value to be converted.

Returns
String type

Immediate Window Sample
? CStr(12)
? CStr(1+2)

SEE ALSO   CCur, CDbl, CInt, CLng, CSng, CVar, Format, DefStr

CurDir, CurDir$

Returns the path for a specified drive

Description
This function, if passed no argument, will return the path of the selected drive. If passed a string with a drive letter, it returns the path of the requested drive.

NOT AVAILABLE IN VB SCRIPT

Syntax
CurDir$[(drive$)] CurDir[(drive$)]

Parameters

drive$ Optional. Single-letter string to indicate desired drive.

Returns

Variant type

Immediate Window Sample

```
? CurDir
? CurDir("C")
```

SEE ALSO   ChDir, ChDrive, MkDir, RmDir

CVar

Converts the given expression to a Variant

Description

This will convert a specific value to a Variant data type.

NOT AVAILABLE IN VB SCRIPT

Syntax

```
CVar(expression)
```

Parameters

expression   Required. Value to be converted.

Returns

Variant type

Immediate Window Sample

```
? CVar(1)
? CVar("Hello")
? CVar(Int(5/2))
```

SEE ALSO   CCur, CDbl, CInt, CLng, CSng, CStr, DefVar

CVDate

Converts the current expression into a Date type variable

Description

With this command, you can convert any number of data types and string formats into an actual date. A Date is a 64-bit (8-byte) value that may be between January 1, 1000, and December 31, 9999.

NOT AVAILABLE IN VB SCRIPT

Syntax

CVDate(expression)

Parameters

expression   Required. Value to be converted.

Returns

Date type

Immediate Window Sample

```
? CVDate("11/2/97")
? CVDate("November 2, 1997")
```

SEE ALSO   DateAdd, DateDiff, DatePart, DateSerial, DateValue, Date, Time, Format, Now, Day, IsDate, Month, Weekday

Date

Sets the current Date in the system

Description

This function sets the actual system date, so be careful with its use.

AVAILABLE IN VB SCRIPT

Syntax
```
Date = date
```

Parameters
date   Required. Date data type.

Returns
N/A

Immediate Window Sample
```
Date = #August 12, 1997#
```

SEE ALSO   CVDate, DateAdd, DateDiff, DatePart, DateSerial, DateValue, Time, Format, Now, Day, IsDate, Month, Weekday

Date, Date$

Returns the current date as a Date type or a String type

Description
This routine returns the current date of the system.

NOT AVAILABLE IN VB SCRIPT

Syntax
```
Date$ Date
```

Parameters
N/A

Returns
Variant or String type

Immediate Window Sample
```
? Date
```

SEE ALSO   CVDate, DateAdd, DateDiff, DatePart, DateSerial, DateValue, Date, Time, Format, Now, Day, IsDate, Month, Weekday

DateAdd

Adds a specified amount to the Date type variable passed to it.

Description

The format returned by DateAdd is determined by the Control Panel settings. Intervals may be year (yyyy), quarter (q), month (m), day of year (y), day (d), weekday (w), week (ww), hour (h), minute (n), or second (s).

AVAILABLE IN VB SCRIPT

Syntax

```
DateAdd(interval$, number%, dateVar)
```

Parameters

interval   Required. Interval to add to the specified datetime.

number   Required. Multiplier of the interval.

dateVar   Required. The Date type to be used as the base of the addition.

Returns

Date type

Immediate Window Sample

```
? DateAdd("m", 1, Now)
? DateAdd("ww", 2, Now)
? DateAdd("h", 5, Now)
```

SEE ALSO   CVDate, DateDiff, DatePart, DateSerial, DateValue, Date, Time, Format, Now, Day, IsDate, Month, Weekday

DateDiff

Determines the difference between two dates in units of the interval passed to it

Description

This function returns the number of intervals between the two periods. Intervals may be year (yyyy), quarter (q), month (m), day of year (y), day (d), weekday (w), week (ww), hour (h), minute (n), or second (s).

AVAILABLE IN VB SCRIPT

Syntax

```
DateDiff(interval$, date1, date2[,firstdayof-
week[,firstweekofyear]])
```

Parameters

interval   Required. Interval to add to the specified datetime.

date1, date2   Required. The Date type.

firstdayofweek   Optional. Specifies first day of week (1=Sunday (default), 2=Monday, and so on).

firstweekofyear   Optional. Specifies the first week of the year (1=Jan 1. (default))

Returns

Variant type

Immediate Window Sample

```
? DateDiff("d",Now,#1/1/2000#)
```

SEE ALSO   CVDate, DateAdd, DatePart, DateSerial, DateValue, Date, Time, Format, Now, Day, IsDate, Month, Weekday

DatePart

Returns the part of the date specified by the interval string

Description

Intervals may be year (yyyy), quarter (q), month (m), day of year (y), day (d), weekday (w), week (ww), hour (h), minute (n), or second (s).

Syntax
```
DatePart(interval$, date)
```

Parameters
interval$ Required. Interval to derive from the specified datetime.

date   Required. The Date type to be used as the base of the conversion.

Returns
Variant

Immediate Window Sample
```
? DatePart("m",Now)
```

SEE ALSO   CVDate, DateAdd, DateDiff, DateSerial, DateValue, Date, Time, Format, Now, Day, IsDate, Month, Weekday

DateSerial

Returns a Date type for the specified values

Description
This routine allows the quick creation of a date from three integer values.

AVAILABLE IN VB SCRIPT

Syntax
```
DateSerial(year%, month%, day%)
```

Parameters
year%, **month%**, **day%**   Required. Integers.

Returns
Variant type

Immediate Window Sample
`? DateSerial(1997,8,1)`

SEE ALSO DateAdd, DateDiff, DatePart, DateValue, Date, Time, Format, Now, Day, IsDate, Month, Weekday, CVDate

DateValue

Converts an expression to a Date type

Description
This function works very similarly to the CVDate function.

AVAILABLE IN VB SCRIPT

Syntax
`DateValue(datestring$)`

Parameters
datestring$ An expression representing a date

Returns
Variant type

Immediate Window Sample
`? DateValue("August 15, 1997")`

SEE ALSO DateAdd, DateDiff, DatePart, DateSerial, Date, Time, Format, Now, Day, IsDate, Month, Weekday, CVDate, #

Day

Returns the day value from the passed date argument

Description
The returned day value will be an integer between 1 and 31 representing the day of the month.

AVAILABLE IN VB SCRIPT

Syntax
Day(dateVariant)

Parameters
dateVariant   Required. Date to be used to retrieve the requested day.

Returns
Integer type

Immediate Window Sample
? Day(Now)

SEE ALSO   DateAdd, DateDiff, DatePart, DateSerial, DateValue, Date, Time, Format, Now, IsDate, Month, Weekday, CVDate

---

DDB

Returns a depreciation value of an asset

Description
Depreciation is determined by use of a double-declining balance method unless another factor is specified using the factor parameter. The double-declining balance uses the number 2 for the factor parameter.

AVAILABLE IN VB SCRIPT

Syntax
DDB(cost@, salvage@, Life%, period%[, factor])

Parameters
cost@   Required. Initial cost of asset as Double type.

salvage@   Required. Value at end of useful life as Double type.

life@   Required. Length of useful life as Double type.

period@ Required. Period for which depreciation is calculated as Double type.

factor@ Optional. Rate that balance declines (default=2) as Variant type.

Returns
Double type

Immediate Window Sample
? DDB(10000,500,24,12)

SEE ALSO FV, IPmt, IIR, MIRR, NPer, NPV, Pmt, PPmt, PV, Rate, SLN, SYD

Declare

Creates a reference to a procedure or function in an external DLL

Description
The Libname$ is the name of the DLL to be called. The .DLL extension is optional and will be added automatically if omitted. The procedure name is case sensitive, so make sure the name you use in the declaration is exact. Visual Basic includes the API Text Viewer application that contains VB declarations for all Win32 API calls.

NOT AVAILABLE IN VB SCRIPT

Syntax
```
Declare Sub Procname Lib Libname$ [Alias
aliasname$][(ar-gList)] Declare Function procname
[Lib Libname$] [Alias aliasname$][(arg-List)]
[As type]
```

Parameters
Procname Required. Case-sensitive name must match function name unless given in aliasname parameter.

Libname$ Name of library containing Sub or Function.

aliasname Name or ordinal number of the specified routine.

arg-List   Any parameters and their types that must be passed.

Returns
N/A

Immediate Window Sample
N/A

User Tip
The aliasname$ can also be an ordinal number to call the index of a
DLL routine. For example, setting the aliasname$ to "#2" will call
the second routine stored in the DLL.

SEE ALSO   Call

DefBool

Specifies default data types for arguments to Boolean for specified
settings

Description
This command can be used to automatically set the data type of a
variable based on the starting of the name. For example, "DefBool
B" would make any new untyped variables that begin with the
letter "B" Boolean type. The statement "BNum = 4" would be a
Boolean type. This is used at the module level.

AVAILABLE IN VB SCRIPT

Syntax
```
DefBool letterRange[, letterRange]...
```

Parameters
letterRange   Range can be a single letter or from–to such as A–Z

Returns
N/A

Immediate Window Sample
N/A

SEE ALSO DefDbl, DefInt, DefLng, DefSng, DefStr, DefVar, CBool, CCur, CDbl, CInt, CLng, CSng, CStr, CVar

DefByte

Specifies default data types for arguments to Bytes for specified settings

Description

This command can be used to automatically set the data type of a variable based on the starting of the name. For example, "DefByte B" would make any new untyped variables that begin with the letter "B" Byte type. The statement "BNum = 4" would be a Byte type. This is used at the module level.

AVAILABLE IN VB SCRIPT

Syntax

```
DefByte letterRange[, letterRange]...
```

Parameters

letterRange Range can be a single letter or from–to such as A–Z

Returns

N/A

Immediate Window Sample

N/A

SEE ALSO DefDbl, DefInt, DefLng, DefSng, DefStr, DefVar

DefCur

Specifies default data types for arguments to Currency for specified settings

Description

This command can be used to automatically set the data type of a variable based on the starting of the name. For example, "DefCur C" would make any new untyped variables that begin with the letter "C" Currency type. The statement "CNum = 4" would be a Currency type. This is used at the module level.

AVAILABLE IN VB SCRIPT

Syntax

```
DefCur letterRange[, letterRange]...
```

Parameters

letterRange   Range can be a single letter or from–to such as A–Z

Returns

N/A

Immediate Window Sample

N/A

SEE ALSO   DefDbl, DefInt, DefLng, DefSng, DefStr, DefVar

DefDbl

Specifies default data types for arguments to Double for specified settings

Description

This command can be used to automatically set the data type of a variable based on the starting of the name. For example, "DefDbl Z" would make any new untyped variables that begin with the letter "Z" Double type. The statement "ZNum = 4" would be a Double type. This is used at the module level.

AVAILABLE IN VB SCRIPT

Syntax

```
DefDbl letterRange[, letterRange]...
```

Parameters

letterRange   Range can be a single letter or from–to such as A–Z

Returns

N/A

Immediate Window Sample

N/A

SEE ALSO   DefBool, DefByte, DefCur, DefInt, DefLng, DefObj, DefSng, DefStr, DefVar

DefInt

Specifies default data types for arguments to Integer for specified settings

Description

This command can be used to automatically set the data type of a variable based on the starting of the name. For example, "DefInt i" would make any new untype variables that begin with the letter "i" Integer type. The statement "iNum = 4" would create an Int type. This is used at the module level.

AVAILABLE IN VB SCRIPT

Syntax

```
DefInt letterRange[, letterRange]...
```

Parameters

letterRange   Range can be a single letter or from–to such as A–Z

Returns

N/A

Immediate Window Sample

N/A

SEE ALSO   DefBool, DefByte, DefCur, DefDbl, DefLng, DefObj, DefSng, DefStr, DefVar

DefLng

Specifies default data types for arguments to Long for specified settings

Description

This command can be used to automatically set the data type of a variable based on the starting of the name. For example, "DefLng L" would make any new untyped variables that begin with the letter "L" Long type. The statement "LNum = 4" would be a Long type. This is used at the module level.

AVAILABLE IN VB SCRIPT

Syntax
```
DefLng letterRange[, letterRange]...
```

Parameters
letterRange   Range can be a single letter or from–to such as A–Z

Returns
N/A

Immediate Window Sample
N/A

SEE ALSO   DefBool, DefByte, DefCur, DefDbl, DefInt, DefObj, DefSng, DefStr, DefVar

DefObj

Specifies default data types for arguments to Objects for specified settings

Description

This command can be used to automatically set the data type of a variable based on the starting of the name. For example, "DefObj O" would make any new untyped variables that begin with the letter

"O" Object type. The statement "Dim oExcel" would be an Object type. This is used at the module level.

AVAILABLE IN VB SCRIPT

Syntax
```
DefObj letterRange[, letterRange]...
```

Parameters
letterRange   Range can be a single letter or from–to such as A–Z

Returns
N/A

Immediate Window Sample
N/A

SEE ALSO   DefBool, DefByte, DefCur, DefDbl, DefInt, DefLng, DefSng, DefStr, DefVar

---

DefSng

Specifies default data types for arguments to Singles for specified settings

Description
This command can be used to automatically set the data type of a variable based on the starting of the name. For example, "DefSng G" would make any new untyped variables that begin with the letter "G" Single type. The statement "GNum = 4" would be a Single type. This is used at the module level.

AVAILABLE IN VB SCRIPT

Syntax
```
DefSng letterRange[, letterRange]...
```

Parameters
letterRange   Range can be a single letter or from–to such as A–Z

Returns

N/A

Immediate Window Sample

N/A

SEE ALSO   DefCur, DefDbl, DefInt, DefLng, DefStr, DefVar

DefStr

Specifies default data types for arguments to Strings for specified settings

Description

This command can be used to automatically set the data type of a variable based on the starting of the name. For example, "DefStr S" would make any new untyped variables that begin with the letter "S" String type. The statement "sName = "Joe"" would be a String type. This is used at the module level.

AVAILABLE IN VB SCRIPT

Syntax

```
DefStr letterRange[, letterRange]...
```

Parameters

letterRange   Range can be a single letter or from–to such as A–Z

Returns

N/A

Immediate Window Sample

N/A

SEE ALSO   DefCur, DefDbl, DefInt, DefLng, DefSng, DefVar

DefVar

Specifies default data types for arguments to Variants for specified settings

Description

This command can be used to automatically set the data type of a variable based on the starting of the name. For example, "DefVar U-W" would make any new untyped variables that begin with the letter "U" through "V" a Variant type. The statement "VNum = 4" would be a Variant type. This is used at the module level.

AVAILABLE IN VB SCRIPT

Syntax
```
DefVar letterRange[, letterRange]...
```

Parameters

letterRange   Range can be a single letter or from–to such as A–Z

Returns

N/A

Immediate Window Sample

N/A

SEE ALSO   DefCur, DefDbl, DefInt, DefLng, DefSng, DefStr

Dim

Defines a variable

Description

This defines the variable and can set the type of the variable either with the As keyword or through the variable suffixes (such as $, %, etc.). This command cannot be used in the Immediate window.

AVAILABLE IN VB SCRIPT

Syntax

```
Dim [Shared] name [As [New] type][, name [As [New]
type]]
```

2

Parameters

name   Permitted names include alphanumerics and basic symbols (such as the underscore), but no spaces

type   Required if As keyword is used. Can be type such as Double, Integer, Byte, String, Object, Single, Currency, or Long.

Returns

N/A

Immediate Window Sample

N/A

User Tip

Since Dim cannot be used in the Immediate window, define variables in the Immediate window implicitly (that is, i=5), by use of the conversion functions (that is, a=CStr(12)), or by use of the array command (that is, a = array(3,5,9)).

SEE ALSO   Global, Option Base, ReDim, Static, Type, Private, Public, Const, VarType

---

Dir, Dir$

Returns the name of the file or path that matches the pattern passed in the argument

Description

The first call to this function must contain the requested pattern. If the next call omits the pattern argument, the next file or path that matches the original pattern will be returned. An empty string will be returned if none matching the pattern is found.

NOT AVAILABLE IN VB SCRIPT

Syntax

For the first call to Dir$ for a pattern:

```
Dir$(pattern$[,attributes]) Dir(pattern$)
```

For each successive call for the same pattern:

```
Dir$ Dir
```

Parameters

pattern$ Any path or filename. May include wildcards.

Returns

String type

Immediate Window Sample

```
? Dir("C:\WINDOWS\WIN.INI")
? Dir("C:\WINDOWS\*.INI)
? Dir()
```

User Tip

This function may be used to effectively create a routine to determine if a file exists.

SEE ALSO   CurDir$, ChDir, ChDrive

Do...Loop

Cycles through a loop until the necessary condition is met

Description

The Do...Loop structure can continue cycling while a condition is True (While) or until it is True (Until). Favor the Do...Loop structure over the While...Wend statements.

AVAILABLE IN VB SCRIPT

Syntax

To test the condition at the top of a loop:

```
Do [{While I Until} condition] [statements] [Exit Do]
[statements] Loop
```

To test the condition at the bottom of the loop:

```
Do [statements] Loop [{While I Until} condition]
```

2

Parameters

condition   Required. Boolean condition that may be evaluated to either True or False.

Returns

N/A

Immediate Window Sample

```
i=0 : Do While i < 5 : ? i : i=i+1 : Loop
i=0 : Do Until i > 5 : ? i : i=i+1 : Loop
```

SEE ALSO   Exit, For...Next, While...Wend

DoEvents

Pauses to allow the system to process events

Description

A loop that is doing a great number of operations provides few processing resources for the rest of the system for tasks such as screen updates. This command pauses for the system to process other tasks.

NOT AVAILABLE IN VB SCRIPT

Syntax

```
DoEvents() 'function
DoEvents 'statement
```

Parameters

N/A

Returns

N/A

Immediate Window Sample

DoEvents

User Tip

When creating program status indicators, you will often need to use the DoEvents command to pause for the system to redraw text boxes, progress bars, and so on. This will slow execution, but will allow users to see what progress has taken place.

SEE ALSO Stop, End

End

Stops execution or ends a definition of a Function, If structure, Select statement, Subroutine, or Type definition

Description

The End command is used to terminate either execution or a definition. Only the End If statement will automatically insert the necessary space when it is typed (automatically converting "endif" to "End If").

NOT AVAILABLE IN VB SCRIPT

Syntax

End [Function | If | Select | Sub | Type]

Parameters

N/A

Returns

N/A

Immediate Window Sample

End

User Tip

Use the End command by itself to completely stop execution of a program, such as when the user selects the Exit option on the File menu.

SEE ALSO   Function, If...Then...Else, Select Case, Stop, Sub, Type

Environ, Environ$

Returns information on the current environment

Description

The operating system stores a great deal of information available through this function. These variables include such information as the Path statement, the Prompt information, the Temp directory, and so on. Each returned string begins with the environmental variable, followed by an = sign, followed by the current setting.

NOT AVAILABLE IN VB SCRIPT

Syntax

```
Environ$({entry-name$ | entry-position%})
Environ({entry-name$ | entry-position%})
```

Parameters

entry-name$ The name of the environmental variable to retrieve

entry-position%   The index of the environmental variable

Returns

String type

Immediate Window Sample

```
? Environ("path")
? Environ(1)
? Environ(2)
? Environ(3)
```

SEE ALSO   Command, Command$

EOF

Returns the End-of-File condition

Description

This function may be used effectively with a Do...Loop to process a file. The Immediate window example requires a file TEST.TXT located at the root of C to function properly. Change the file and path names to use a different file.

NOT AVAILABLE IN VB SCRIPT

Syntax

```
EOF(file-number)
```

Parameters

file-number The current file number assigned when the file was opened

Returns

Integer type

Immediate Window Sample

```
Open "C:\test.txt" for Input as #1 : ? EOF(1) :_
Close #1
```

User Tip

You may check this function when a file is initially opened with a True condition indicating that the file is empty.

SEE ALSO   Close, Get, Input #, Line Input #, Loc, LOF, Open

Eqv

Logical equivalence operator

Description

This operator essentially performs a bitwise And on two numeric expressions.

AVAILABLE IN VB SCRIPT

Syntax

```
a Eqv b
```

Parameters

a, **b**   Required. Numeric expressions.

Returns

Boolean type

Immediate Window Sample

```
? 8 Eqv 8
? True Eqv False
```

SEE ALSO   And, Or, Imp, Xor, True, False

Erase

Clears the current contents of the array

Description

This clears the values of fixed-size arrays and releases the memory of a dynamic array.

AVAILABLE IN VB SCRIPT

Syntax

```
Erase arrayname [, arrayname]
```

Parameters

arrayname   Required. The name of the array to be cleared.

Returns

N/A

Immediate Window Sample

```
myArray = array(1,5,7,9)
? myArray(2)
Erase myArray
? myArray(2)
```

SEE ALSO   Dim, ReDim, Array

Err Object

Contains complete information about an error that has occurred

Description
The Clear method will clear the current error, while the Description and Number properties describe the error itself. The Err object is mostly used in conjunction with an On Error routine within a procedure or function.

NOT AVAILABLE IN VB SCRIPT

Syntax
```
Err.Raise errornum
```

Parameters
errornum   Required. Integer with error code to be generated.

Returns
N/A

Immediate Window Sample
```
Err.Clear Err.Raise 6
```

SEE ALSO   Erl, Error, Error$, On Error GoTo, Resume

Error

Generates an error of the specified type in the system

Description
This statement will cause the Visual Basic system to receive an error of the type specified.

NOT AVAILABLE IN VB SCRIPT

Syntax
```
Error errorcode%
```

Parameters

errorcode%   Required. Integer error code number.

Returns

N/A

Immediate Window Sample

```
Error 6
```

User Tip

You can use these errors yourself when debugging by generating exactly the type error you need to document problems the user is having.

SEE ALSO   Err, Error$, On Error GoTo, Resume

Error, Error$

Returns the error message that corresponds to the passed argument

Description

This function returns the technical English explanation of the error type passed in the errorcode argument.

AVAILABLE IN VB SCRIPT

Syntax

```
Error$[(errorcode%)] Error[(errorcode%)]
```

Parameters

errorcode%   Required. Integer representing an error code number.

Returns

String type

Immediate Window Sample

```
? Error$(6)
```

SEE ALSO   Err, Error, On Error GoTo, Resume

Event

Creates a user-defined event

Description
Once you define an event, the RaiseEvent command may generate that event to activate the routine. This command is not available in VBA or VB Script, only in the complete Visual Basic development environment.

NOT AVAILABLE IN VB SCRIPT

Syntax
```
[Public] Event procedurename [arglist]
```

Parameters
procedurename   Required. Any permitted name for the event.

arglist   Optional. Any arguments that are to be passed to the event.

Returns
N/A

Immediate Window Sample
N/A

SEE ALSO   Sub, Function, Property Let, Property Get, Property Set

Exit

Terminates the current operation before the conditions are complete

Description
You can use the Exit Do to exit a Do...Loop before the final conditions have been met. The same is possible with For...Next loops, subroutines, and functions.

AVAILABLE IN VB SCRIPT

Syntax

```
Exit Do
Exit For
Exit Function
Exit Sub
```

Parameters

N/A

Returns

N/A

Immediate Window Sample

N/A

SEE ALSO   Do...Loop, For...Next, Function, Sub

Exp

Raises the base of natural logarithms (e) to a specified power

Description

The function (known as an antilogarithm) returns a Double type based on the results of the passed exponent. The constant e is approximately 2.718282.

AVAILABLE IN VB SCRIPT

Syntax

```
Exp(power)
```

Parameters

power   Required. Double type to be used as the exponent.

Returns

Double type

Immediate Window Sample

```
? exp(1)
? exp(20)
```

SEE ALSO Log

False

Logical False

Description
This constant can be used in most expressions, bitwise operations, and comparisons.

AVAILABLE IN VB SCRIPT

Syntax
```
False
```

Parameters
N/A

Returns
N/A

Immediate Window Sample
```
? (2=2) = False
? (2=2) = True
```

SEE ALSO And, Or, Imp, Eqv, Xor, True

FileAttr

Returns the mode (input, output, and so on) of the specified file

Description
This function can be used to determine the current attributes of an open file. The mode can be input (1), output (2), random (4), append (8), or binary (32).

NOT AVAILABLE IN VB SCRIPT

Syntax
```
FileAttr(filenumber%[, infotype%])
```

Parameters
filenumber%   Required. Any valid file number ID.

infotype%   Optional. On 32-bit systems, must be equal to 1. On 16-bit systems, a type 2 will return a system file handle.

Returns
Long type

Immediate Window Sample
```
Open "C:\test.txt" for Input as #1 : ? FileAttr(1)_
: Close #1
```

SEE ALSO   Open, Input #, Print #, Close

FileCopy

Copies a file from the source to the destination

Description
This routine acts as the traditional file-copy operating system call and makes a duplicate of the file (with path) described in the source$ to the file (with path) denoted in the second string.

NOT AVAILABLE IN VB SCRIPT

Syntax
```
FileCopy source$, dest$
```

Parameters
source$**, **dest$ Required. Strings containing paths and filenames.

Returns
N/A

Immediate Window Sample
```
FileCopy "C:\test.txt" "C:\testdup.txt"
```

User Tip

Use of the FileCopy command is an effective way to create database templates. Since it is difficult to dynamically construct a database, you can keep a blank structured database in the program folder. When you need a copy, use FileCopy to create it.

SEE ALSO ChDir, ChDrive, CurDir, Open, Close, MkDir, RmDir, Kill

FileDateTime

Returns the date and time when a specified file was last modified

Description

Simply passing a valid filename and path will return the last modified date of any accessible file.

NOT AVAILABLE IN VB SCRIPT

Syntax

```
FileDateTime(filename$)
```

Parameters

filename$ Required. Any valid path and filename.

Returns

Variant (Date) type

Immediate Window Sample

```
? FileDateTime "C:\test.txt"
```

SEE ALSO GetAttr, FileLen, ChDir, ChDrive, CurDir, Open, Close, MkDir, RmDir, Kill

FileLen

Returns the length in bytes of a particular file

Description

This routine can determine the length of any file available to the system. The file does not need to be opened with any of the disk-access commands to get its length.

NOT AVAILABLE IN VB SCRIPT

Syntax

```
FileLen(filename$)
```

Parameters

filename$ Required. Any valid path and filename.

Returns

Long type

Immediate Window Sample

```
? FileLen "C:\test.txt"
```

SEE ALSO   FileDateTime, GetAttr, ChDir, ChDrive, CurDir, Open, Close, MkDir, RmDir, Kill

---

Fix

Returns an integer of the passed value

Description

This function works almost exactly like the Int( ) function except when concerning negative numbers. Fix returns the first negative number greater than or equal to the passed value. Int( ) returns the first negative number that is less than or equal to the value. Fix(–1.4) would return the value –1, while Int(–1.4) would return the value –2.

AVAILABLE IN VB SCRIPT

Syntax

```
Fix(numericExpression)
```

Parameters

numericExpression   Required. Any valid numeric expression.

Returns

Integer type

Immediate Window Sample

```
? Fix(1.4)
? Fix(-1.4)
```

SEE ALSO   CInt, Int

For Each...Next

Cycles through an entire collection of objects or items in an array

Description

The For Each...Next structure will cycle through all of the elements, even if they are not in numeric order. In an object collection, the element variable is set to reference the current object.

AVAILABLE IN VB SCRIPT

Syntax

```
For Each element In group [statements] Next [element]
```

Parameters

element   Required. A variable that will hold the current reference to the selected object or array item.

group   An array or collection reference.

Returns

N/A

Immediate Window Sample

```
myArray = array(5,8,10,98)
For Each myItem in myArray : ? myItem : Next
```

SEE ALSO   Do...Loop, Exit, While...Wend, For...Next, CreateObject, GetObject

For...Next

Loops until necessary value is reached

Description
The For...Next structure will cycle through the statements in the loop until the endvalue is reached.

AVAILABLE IN VB SCRIPT

Syntax
```
For counter = startvalue To endvalue [Step increment]
    [statements]
    [Exit For]
    [statements]
Next [counter][, counter]...
```

Parameters
counter   Required. Variable that keeps the current increment.

startvalue   Required. Begin value of loop.

endvalue   Required. End value of loop.

step   Optional. Amount that counter is increased every time through the loop.

Returns
N/A

Immediate Window Sample
```
For i = 1 to 10 : ? i : Next i
For i=10 to 1 step -1 : ? i : Next
```

SEE ALSO   Do...Loop, Exit, While...Wend, For Each...Next

Format, Format$

Returns a string formatted in a number of ways including string, date, time, currency, and other formats

Description
The Format command is one of the most powerful commands for easily and quickly generating output in a desired format. Use the # within the editPattern to indicate a placeholder.

AVAILABLE IN VB SCRIPT

Syntax
Format$(numericExpression, editPattern$)

Parameters
numericExpression   Required. Valid expression including dates.

editPattern$ Required. Pattern required for output.

Returns
Variant or String type

Immediate Window Sample
```
? Format(Now, "hh:mm:ss AMPM")
? Format(Now, "h:m:s")
? Format(Now, "mmm d yyyy")
? Format(2534.64,"##,##0")
? Format(2534.64,"##,##0.00")
? Format(2534.64,"##,###.##")
? Format(-2534.64,"$##,##0.00;($##,##0.00)")
```

SEE ALSO   DateSerial, Now, Str, Str$, TimeSerial, CVDate, Val, CStr, &, DateValue

FreeFile

Returns the next valid free file number

Description

This function will return the next available number for use as a file. Use this command if a program needs to manually specify the index number of a file to be opened. If you've been letting the system supply the file number, checking this value will reveal how many files have been opened this session.

NOT AVAILABLE IN VB SCRIPT

Syntax

```
FreeFile
```

Parameters

N/A

Returns

Integer type

Immediate Window Sample

```
? FreeFile
```

SEE ALSO Open, Close, Print #, Input #, ChDir, ChDrive, CurDir, Get, Put, GetAttr, MkDir, RmDir

FreeLocks

Allows background processing to occur to keep open dynasets current

Description

If processing is too intense, calling this function will activate any processing required on dynasets to keep them current. This routine is obsolete and included in Visual Basic only for backward compatibility.

NOT AVAILABLE IN VB SCRIPT

Syntax

```
FreeLocks
```

Parameters
N/A

Returns
N/A

Immediate Window Sample
N/A

SEE ALSO   DoEvents

Function...End Function

Creates a function in a module or form

Description
This command allows definition of a function that may include the types of arguments that will be received by the function as well as the arguments that will be returned.

AVAILABLE IN VB SCRIPT

Syntax
```
[Static] [Private] Function function-name [(argu-
ments)]
[As type] [Static var[,var]...] [Dim var[,var]...]
    [statements]
    [function-name = expression]
    [Exit Function]
    [statements]
    [function-name = expression]
End Function
```

Parameters
arguments   Required. Any arguments to be received by the function.

Returns
Any defined type

Immediate Window Sample

N/A

User Tip

The value returned by the function is set by setting the name of the function itself to the value. To return the value 5 from the function myFunction, the code "myFunction = 5" would appear within the body.

SEE ALSO   End, Exit, Sub

FV

Returns the future value of an annuity

Description

The value that is returned is calculated from the period, the fixed payments, and the fixed interest rate.

NOT AVAILABLE IN VB SCRIPT

Syntax

```
FV(rate!, numPeriods%, payment@, presentValue@, when-
Due%)
```

Parameters

rate!   Required. Double type of interest rate per period.

numPeriods%   Required. Integer of total number of payments.

payment@   Required. Double type of the amount of each payment.

presentValue@   Optional. Variant of the present value.

whenDue%   Optional. 0 = Payments due at end of period, 1 = beginning of the period.

Returns

Double type

Immediate Window Sample
```
? FV(.0081,48,-1500.75)
```

SEE ALSO   DDB, IPmt, IIR, MIRR, NPer, NPV, Pmt, PPmt, PV, Rate, SLN, SYD

Get

Retrieves information from an open file and places it in a variable

Description
The Get command reads the data usually written into the file by a Put statement. All data types are supported.

NOT AVAILABLE IN VB SCRIPT

Syntax
```
Get [#]filenumber%,[position&], recordbuffer
```

Parameters
filenumber%   Required. Any valid open file number.

position&   Optional. Specifies record number in a Random file or a byte number in a Binary file where writing should occur.

recordbuffer   Required. A valid variable that will have its contents read from the file.

Returns
N/A

Immediate Window Sample
```
Open "C:\test.txt" for Input as #1 : Get #1,a :_
Close #1
```

SEE ALSO   LOF, Open, Put, Type, FileLen, Input #, Line Input #

GetAttr

Returns the attributes of a given file

Description

As opposed to FileAttr, which returns information about open files, GetAttr returns such information as Normal (0), ReadOnly (1), Hidden (2), System (4), Directory (16), or Archive (32) designations about a file on the disk.

NOT AVAILABLE IN VB SCRIPT

Syntax

```
GetAttr(fileName$)
```

Parameters

fileName$ Required. A valid path and filename.

Returns

Integer type

Immediate Window Sample

```
? GetAttr("c:\test.txt")
```

SEE ALSO   FileDateTime, FileLen, FileAttr, Open, Close, EOF, LOF, Loc

Global

Declares a variable globally available to all forms and modules in a project

Description

The Global command can only be used in a module. To make a method or property of a form available to the project, use the Public keyword.

NOT AVAILABLE IN VB SCRIPT

Syntax

For declaring the data type of a simple variable:

```
Global name [As [New] type][, name [As [New] type]]
```

For declaring an array:

```
Global name[(subscript-range)][As [New] type]
[, name[(subscript-range)][As [New] type]
```

Parameters

name   Permitted names including alphanumerics and basic symbols (such as the underscore), but no spaces.

type   Required. Can be type such as Double, Integer, Byte, String, Object, Single, Currency, or Long.

Returns

N/A

Immediate Window Sample

N/A

SEE ALSO   Const, Dim, Option Base, Static, Public, Private

GoSub...Return

This command can be used to jump within a subroutine or function to a piece of code

Description

Using the GoSub breaks the flow of the program by allowing in-subroutine jumps. The LineLabel or Linenumber sets the anchors for the top of the sub-subroutines.

NOT AVAILABLE IN VB SCRIPT

Syntax

```
GoSub {LineLabel | linenumber}
{LineLabel: | Linenumber} : [statement-block] : Return
```

Parameters

LineLabel | linenumber   Required. Numeric or alphanumeric anchor that a GoSub command can jump to.

Returns

N/A

Immediate Window Sample

N/A

User Tip

Try to avoid the use of GoSub and GoTo commands—they remain in Visual Basic mostly for compatibility with older versions. They make code difficult to read and expensive to maintain.

SEE ALSO   On...GoSub, Sub

GoTo

This command will jump execution within a procedure or function

Description

Use the GoTo command to jump to an out-of-sequence set of code.

NOT AVAILABLE IN VB SCRIPT

Syntax

```
GoTo [linenumber | linelabel}
```

Parameters

linelabel | linenumber   Required. Numeric or alphanumeric anchor that a GoSub command can jump to.

Returns

N/A

Immediate Window Sample

N/A

User Tip

Try to avoid the use of GoSub and GoTo commands, as they remain in Visual Basic mostly for compatibility with older versions. They make code difficult to read and expensive to maintain.

SEE ALSO   GoSub

Hex, Hex$

Converts a number to its hexadecimal equivalent

Description

This function will create a string containing the hexadecimal (base 16 number) from the passed value. Each value may contain the numbers 0–9 and the letters A–F.

AVAILABLE IN VB SCRIPT

Syntax

Hex$(numericExpression) Hex(numericExpression)

Parameters

numericExpression   Required. Any numeric expression.

Returns

String type

Immediate Window Sample

```
? Hex(9)
? Hex(10)
? Hex(255)
? Hex(256)
```

SEE ALSO   Oct, Oct$

Hour

2

Returns the hour portion of a date and time value

Description
The returned hour value will be an integer between 0 and 23 representing the hour of the day.

AVAILABLE IN VB SCRIPT

Syntax
```
Hour(dateVariant)
```

Parameters
dateVariant   The date that the hour is to be extracted from

Returns
Integer type

Immediate Window Sample
```
? Hour(Now)
```

SEE ALSO   Now, TimeSerial, TimeValue, Time, Minute, Second

If...Then...Elseif...End If

Conditional execution of statements

Description
The If...Then structure allows evaluation of conditions for a change in the program flow. If the statements to be executed are placed on a single line, the End If statements can be eliminated. However, for code clarity, it is often a good idea to include them.

AVAILABLE IN VB SCRIPT

Syntax

```
If condition-1 Then
    [actions-1]
[ElseIf condition-2 Then]
    [actions-2]
[ElseIf condition-n Then]
    [actions-n]
[Else]
    [else-actions]
End If
```

Parameters

conditions   Required. Boolean expressions.

Returns

N/A

Immediate Window Sample

```
a = 1
If a = 1 then ? "Equal" else ? "Not equal" end if
a = 2
If a = 1 then ? "Equal" else ? "Not equal" end if
```

SEE ALSO   If...Then...Else, Select Case, Ilf

Returns one of two values depending on the evaluation of an expression

Description

This function, like Switch, can compactly and quickly return a value based on the evaluation of an expression. The Ilf works very well to substitute Null values.

NOT AVAILABLE IN VB SCRIPT

Syntax

```
IIf(expression, valueIfTrue, valueIfFalse)
```

Parameters

expression   Required. Any expression that can be resolved to a Boolean condition.

valueIfTrue, valueIfFalse   Required. Values to be returned from the function depending on the expression.

Returns

Variant

Immediate Window Sample

```
a=1
? IIf(a=1,"It's true","It's not true")
a=2
? IIf(a=1,"It's true","It's not true")
a=Null
? IIf(IsNull(a),0,a)
```

User Tip

The IIF function requires the Financial DLL. The command is not included with the Visual Basic runtime (VBRUN500.DLL) and must be installed separately if you're shipping a Visual Basic solution to customers.

SEE ALSO   If...Then...Else, Select Case, Choose, Switch

Returns logical implication from two values

Description

Order is important when using the Imp operator, as the bitwise comparison between the two values sets the corresponding bit in the result.

AVAILABLE IN VB SCRIPT

Syntax

```
a Imp b
```

Parameters

a, **b**   Required. Valid numeric expressions.

Returns

Variant

Immediate Window Sample

```
? 1 Imp 0
? 1 Imp 1
? 0 Imp 1
? 0 Imp 0
```

SEE ALSO   And, Or, Eqv, Xor, True, False

Input

Returns a string from the open stream of an Input or Binary file

Description

By use of the Open command, once a file's open, the input stream can be read. The Input command can read directly into the specified variable.

NOT AVAILABLE IN VB SCRIPT

Syntax

```
Input #filenumber, var1[, var2]
```

Parameters

filenumber   Required. File to read input stream.

var1   Required. Variable name to read input.

Returns

N/A

Immediate Window Sample

```
Open "c:\test.txt" for Input as #1 : Input #1, a$_
: Close #1
```

User Tip

Since Input # can read a line at a time, it provides the easiest way
to load text-based formats such as SYLK or DIF files.

SEE ALSO   Input, Input$, Write #

Input, Input$

Reads a specified number of bytes from an Input or Binary file

Description

In contrast to the Input # statement made for text files, the Input
function can read a specific number of bytes into memory, which is
ideal for Binary files.

NOT AVAILABLE IN VB SCRIPT

Syntax

```
Input$(inputlength%,[#]filenumber%)
```

Parameters

inputlength%   Required. Number of bytes to read.

filenumber%   Required. Current file number to read from.

Returns

String type

Immediate Window Sample

```
Open "c:\test.txt" for Input as #1 :_
a$ = Input 50,#1 : Close #1
```

User Tip

Use the LOF and the EOF functions to determine the current place
in the file relative to the end.

SEE ALSO   InputB #, Write #, Open, Close, InputB

InputB, InputB$

Reads a specified number of bytes from an Input or Binary file

Description
In contrast to the Input # statement made for text files, the InputB function can read a specific number of bytes into memory, which is ideal for Binary files.

NOT AVAILABLE IN VB SCRIPT

Syntax
```
InputB(inputlength%,[#]filenumber%)
InputB$(inputlength%,[#]filenumber%)
```

Parameters
inputlength%   Required. Number of bytes to read.

filenumber%   Required. Current file number to read from.

Returns
String type

Immediate Window Sample
```
Open "c:\test.txt" for InputB as #1 :_
a$ = InputB 50,#1 : Close #1
```

User Tip
Use the LOF and the EOF functions to determine the current place in the file relative to the end.

SEE ALSO   Input, Input #, Write #

InputBox, InputBox$

Presents an input dialog box that allows the user to enter text information

Description
InputBox functions in much the same way as MsgBox( ). If the user clicks the Cancel button, the returned string will be empty.

AVAILABLE IN VB SCRIPT

2

Syntax
```
InputBox$(msg$[, [title$][, [default$][,xpos%,
ypos%]]])
InputBox(msg$[, [title$][, [default$][, xpos%,
ypos%]]])
```

Parameters
msg$ Required. String that contains the message to display in the input box.

title$ Optional. Title of the dialog box that will be shown.

default$ Optional. Default string to place in the input box.

xpos%, ypos%   Optional. The x and y position where the input box should be displayed.

Returns
String type

Immediate Window Sample
```
a = InputBox("Please enter your name:","Name Entry")
? a
```

SEE ALSO   MsgBox, MsgBox$

InStr

Returns the first place within a string that another string occurs

Description
This function can be used to search for the occurrence of a string and its location within a larger string. The startpos parameter begins the search at a particular position with the string.

AVAILABLE IN VB SCRIPT

Syntax

```
InStr([startpos&], string1$, pattern$)
```

Parameters

startpos&   Optional. The position within the string to begin search.

string1$ Required. String that is to be searched.

pattern$ Required. The pattern string that the function will attempt to locate.

Returns

Long type

Immediate Window Sample

```
? InStr("Hello World from Dan","Dan")
? InStr(3,"Hello World from Dan","World")
```

SEE ALSO   Left$, Right$, Option Compare, Upper, Lower

Int

Converts a number to an Integer data type

Description

This function works almost exactly like the Fix( ) function except when concerning negative numbers. Int returns the first negative number less than or equal to the passed value. Int( ) returns the first negative number less than or equal to the value. Fix(−1.4) would return the value −1, while Int(−1.4) would return the value −2.

AVAILABLE IN VB SCRIPT

Syntax

```
Int(numericExpression)
```

Parameters

numericExpression   Required. Any valid numeric expression.

Returns

Integer type

Immediate Window Sample

```
? Int(1.4)
? Int(-1.4)
```

SEE ALSO   CInt, CStr, CDbl, CVar, CStr, Fix

Returns the interest rate per period calculated from an annuity

Description

The payment is calculated from the values of periodic fixed payments and fixed interest rate. The rate returns the interest rate per period given the other factors.

NOT AVAILABLE IN VB SCRIPT

Syntax

```
IPmt(rate!, currentPeriod%, totalPeriods%, present-
Value@, [FutureValue@, whenDue%])
```

Parameters

rate!   Required. Interest rate for the calculations.

currentPeriod%   Required. Must be greater than 1 and less than totalPeriods.

totalPeriods%   Required.

presentValue@   Required. Current value of payments.

futureValue@   Optional. Final cash value desired.

whenDue%   Optional. End (0) or beginning (1) of payment period.

Returns
Double type

Immediate Window Sample
```
? IPmt(.0081,2,48,20000)
```

SEE ALSO   FV, DDB, IIR, MIRR, NPer, NPV, Pmt, PPmt, PV, Rate, SLN, SYD

IRR

Returns the Return Rate of a series of payments or receipts

Description
This financial function will use an array that must contain at least one negative (payment) and one positive (receipt) value to estimate the Return Rate value. You may include a guess as to the final value which, if omitted, is set to 0.1 (10 percent).

NOT AVAILABLE IN VB SCRIPT

Syntax
```
IRR(valuesArray(),guess!)
```

Parameters
valuesArray   Required. An Array containing positive (receipt) and negative (payment) information.

guess!   Optional. Your estimate of the Return Rate final value.

Returns
Double type

Immediate Window Sample
```
myArray = array(-50000,12000,15000,10000)
? IRR(myArray)
```

SEE ALSO   FV, IPmt, DDB, MIRR, NPer, NPV, Pmt, PPmt, PV, Rate, SLN, SYD

Is

2

Compares two objects

Description
This operator will determine whether both object references point to the same object.

AVAILABLE IN VB SCRIPT

Syntax
```
a Is b
```

Parameters
a, b   Required. Any valid object references.

Returns
Boolean

Immediate Window Sample
```
? A Is B
Set A = B
? A Is B
```

SEE ALSO   GetObject, Set, CreateObject

IsDate

Returns whether the value contains a valid date

Description
This function will check the value passed to it (string, variant, and so on) and determine whether there is either a valid date or time contained in it.

AVAILABLE IN VB SCRIPT

Syntax
```
IsDate(variant)
```

Parameters
variant   Required. Variant or variable data type.

Returns
Boolean type

Immediate Window Sample
```
? IsDate(#1/2/97#)
? IsDate("1/2/97")
? IsDate("")
```

SEE ALSO   IsEmpty, IsNull, IsNumeric, DateAdd, DateDiff, DatePart, DateSerial, DateValue, Date, Time, Format, Now, Month, Weekday, CVDate

IsEmpty

Determines if variable is empty

Description
The IsEmpty function is most often used for user field entry confirmation.

AVAILABLE IN VB SCRIPT

Syntax
```
IsEmpty(variant)
```

Parameters
variant   Required. Variant or variable data type.

Returns
Boolean type

Immediate Window Sample

```
? IsEmpty("a")
? IsEmpty("")
```

SEE ALSO   IsDate, IsNull, IsNumeric, VarType

IsNull

Determines if variable contains a Null

Description

Most often used for database fields, which often contain Nulls.
Nulls cannot be detected with traditional comparison operators
such as "If a=Null then beep."

AVAILABLE IN VB SCRIPT

Syntax

IsNull(variant)

Parameters

variant   Required. Variant or variable data type.

Returns

Boolean type

Immediate Window Sample

```
? IsNull("")
? IsNull(Null)
```

User Tip

You can also use the & command to circumvent database errors.

SEE ALSO   IsDate, IsEmpty, IsNumeric, VarType, Null, IIf

IsNumeric

Determines if variable contains a numeric value

Description
The IsNumeric function is most often used for user field entry confirmation.

AVAILABLE IN VB SCRIPT

Syntax
```
IsNumeric(variant)
```

Parameters
variant   Required. Variant or variable data type.

Returns
Boolean type

Immediate Window Sample
```
? IsNumeric("123")
? IsNumeric("abc")
```

SEE ALSO   IsDate, IsEmpty, IsNull

Kill

Deletes the file specified

Description
The Kill command supports the wildcard characters * (multiple character) and ? (single character) to delete one or more filenames. If an attempt to delete an open file occurs, an error will be generated.

NOT AVAILABLE IN VB SCRIPT

Syntax

```
Kill filename$
```

Parameters

filename$ Required. Any valid path and filename may be used.

Returns

N/A

Immediate Window Sample

```
Kill "c:\test.txt"
```

SEE ALSO   Name, Open, RmDir, MkDir, ChDir, ChDrive, FileLen, EOF

LBound

Returns the lowest subscript available in the array

Description

This function can be used to determine the lower bound of an array. If the array is multidimensional, use the dimension argument to specify the lower bounds to be returned.

AVAILABLE IN VB SCRIPT

Syntax

```
LBound(arrayname[, dimension%])
```

Parameters

arrayname   Required. The name of the array required to determine the limit.

dimension% Optional. The subscript dimension of a multi-dimensional array.

Returns

Long type

Immediate Window Sample
```
myArray = array(6,4,2,5,2,4,6)
? LBound(myArray)
```

SEE ALSO   UBound, Array, Dim, Option Base

LCase, LCase$

Returns an all-lowercase string

Description
This function converts all of the characters in the passed string to lowercase. This function is effective when comparing two strings to make sure the case matches.

AVAILABLE IN VB SCRIPT

Syntax
```
LCase$(expression$) LCase(expression$)
```

Parameters
expression$ Required. Any valid string.

Returns
String type

Immediate Window Sample
```
? LCase("hElLo")
```

SEE ALSO   UCase, UCase$

Left, Left$

Returns a string containing the amount of the left portion of the passed string

Description

This function can be used to take any specified substring from the left to the right and to return it as a separate string.

AVAILABLE IN VB SCRIPT

Syntax

```
Left$(expression$, Length&)
```

Parameters

expression$ Any string expression

Length&   Number of characters to return in the substring

Returns

String

Immediate Window Sample

```
? Left("Hello World",4)
```

SEE ALSO   Mid, Mid$, Right, Right$, InStr$, Format$, LTrim, RTrim, Str, Len, LenB

Len

Returns the length of a specified string

Description

This function is used to determine the length in characters of a string. Either a string itself or a variable containing the string may be passed to this routine.

AVAILABLE IN VB SCRIPT

Syntax

```
Len(variable-name)
```

Parameters

variable-name   Required. Any valid string.

Returns
Long type

Immediate Window Sample
```
a$ = "Hello World"
? len(a)
```

SEE ALSO   LenB, Left, Mid, Mid$, Right, Right$, InStr$, Format$, LTrim, RTrim, Str

LenB

Length of string or variable in bytes

Description
This function is used to determine the length in bytes of a string. Either a string itself or a variable containing the string may be passed to this routine. In contrast to the Len function (which supports Unicode, where each character uses two bytes), the LenB function will return the actual bytes used.

AVAILABLE IN VB SCRIPT

Syntax
```
LenB(variable-name)
```

Parameters
variable-name   Required. Any valid string.

Returns
Long type

Immediate Window Sample
```
a$ = "Hello World"
? LenB(a)
```

SEE ALSO   Left, Right, Mid, ChrB

Let

Sets a variable to a particular value

Description
The Let command is most often implicit when defining variables. It can be used sometimes for code clarification.

AVAILABLE IN VB SCRIPT

Syntax
[Let] variablename = expression

Parameters
variablename Required. A variable name that follows standard naming practices.

expression Required. The expression that will be evaluated to set the variable.

Returns
N/A

Immediate Window Sample
Let i = 1

SEE ALSO   LSet, RSet, Set

Like

Compares a string with a pattern

Description
The Like command supports a number of wildcard characters to create the pattern string to search the primary string. These characters include ? = single character, * = zero or more characters, # = any single digit, [charlist] = any char in charlist, [!charlist] = any single character not in charlist.

AVAILABLE IN VB SCRIPT

Syntax
```
a Like b
```

Parameters
a   Required. String to search.

b   Required. Pattern to search for.

Returns
String type

Immediate Window Sample
```
? "c:\myFile.txt" Like "*.txt"
```

SEE ALSO   Option Compare Text, Option Compare Binary, =, Is, <>, <, >=, <=, Not, And, InStr$

Line Input

Reads a single line from a Sequential file

Description
This command will read directly into a variable a single line delimited by a Chr(13) carriage return or Chr(13) + Chr(10) linefeed and carriage return. The carriage return + linefeed combination is not included with the returned string.

NOT AVAILABLE IN VB SCRIPT

Syntax
```
Line Input #filenumber%, variable
```

Parameters
filenumber%   Required. Any valid open file number.

variable   Required. The String variable that will receive the new information.

Returns
N/A

Immediate Window Sample
```
Line Input#1, a$
```

SEE ALSO   Input #, Print #

Load

Loads a form or control object, but doesn't show it

Description
Use the Load command to read a control or form. The Show method
of the object can then be used to make it visible.

NOT AVAILABLE IN VB SCRIPT

Syntax
For a form:

```
Load form-name
```

For a control:

```
Load control-name(index)
```

Parameters
form-name, **control-name**   Required. Name to reference desired
object.

Returns
N/A

Immediate Window Sample
N/A

SEE ALSO   Unload

LoadPicture

Loads a picture from the specified file for manipulation or placement in a Picture or Image control

Description
The LoadPicture command can be used to load WMF, BMP, or ICO format pictures. This command is not included in VBA.

NOT AVAILABLE IN VB SCRIPT

Syntax
To load a picture into a form or picture box:

```
LoadPicture(picturefile$)
```

To clear a picture from a form or picture box:

```
LoadPicture
```

Parameters
picturefile$ Required. Valid path to a current picture file.

Returns
Variant

Immediate Window Sample
```
a = LoadPicture("c:\windows\rivets.bmp")
```

SEE ALSO   SavePicture

Loc

Sets the current read or write position with the open file

Description

This function will position the current read or write access to an exact record (Random), current byte position divided by 128 (Sequential), or exact byte location (Binary).

NOT AVAILABLE IN VB SCRIPT

Syntax

```
Loc(filenumber%)
```

Parameters

filenumber%   Any valid open file number.

Returns

Long type

Immediate Window Sample

```
? Loc(#1)
```

SEE ALSO   EOF, LOF, Open, FileLen

Lock...Unlock

Locks or unlocks access to parts of the current file for other processes

Description

These commands may be used to control access to a single file to ensure no data is corrupted or destroyed by concurrent reads or writes.

NOT AVAILABLE IN VB SCRIPT

Syntax

```
Lock [#]filenumber%[,startpos&][ To endpos&] :
[statements] : Unlock [#]filenumber%[,startpos&]
[ to endpos&]
```

Parameters

filenumber%   Required. Any valid open file number.

startpos&   Number of first byte or record.

endpos&   Number of last byte or record.

Returns
N/A

Immediate Window Sample
N/A

SEE ALSO   Get, Put, Open, Close, Loc

LOF

Returns the length of a currently open file

Description
This function, when passed a file number, returns the size, in bytes, of the open file.

NOT AVAILABLE IN VB SCRIPT

Syntax
```
LOF([#]filenumber%)
```

Parameters
filenumber%   Required. Any valid file number.

Returns
Long type

Immediate Window Sample
```
? LOF(#1)
```

SEE ALSO   EOF, Loc

Log

Returns the logarithmic expression for the given expression

Description

This function returns the natural log of the passed expression.

AVAILABLE IN VB SCRIPT

Syntax

```
Log(numericExpression)
```

Parameters

numericExpression   Required. Any valid numeric expression.

Returns

Double type

Immediate Window Sample

```
? Log(1.3)
```

SEE ALSO   Exp

LSet

Left-justifies string within the destination and fills the remainder with spaces

Description

This command essentially copies the sourcevariable into the resultvariable, padded with spaces if the resultvariable is longer. For example, if the length of resultvariable is ten characters, a five-character sourcevariable would be copied to it and padded with five space characters. See this example in the Immediate window. This command can also be used to copy from one user-defined variable to another of the same length.

AVAILABLE IN VB SCRIPT

Syntax
```
LSet resultvariable = sourcevariable
```

Parameters
resultvariable   Required. Destination for the new string.

sourcevariable   Left-justified string to copy.

Returns
N/A

Immediate Window Sample
```
a$ = "1234567890"
LSet a$ = "Hello"
? a$ + "<--end">
```

User Tip
You can use LSet for advanced number operations such as a binary file import. LSet will let you copy the actual bytes from one data type to another without conversion. However, using this technique may sacrifice cross-platform portability.

SEE ALSO   Let, RSet, LTrim, LTrim$, Input, Input #

LTrim, LTrim$

Returns a substring with the leading spaces from left to right removed from the passed string

Description
The LTrim function is the complement of the RTrim function, but returns a string taken from left to right. Any spaces on the left side of the string are removed.

AVAILABLE IN VB SCRIPT

Syntax
```
LTrim$(stringExpression$) LTrim(stringExpression$)
```

Parameters
stringExpression$ Required. Any valid string.

Returns
String type

Immediate Window Sample
```
? LTrim(" Hello")
```

SEE ALSO   RTrim, RTrim$, Trim, Trim$, Left, Left$, Right, Right$, Mid$

Me Property

This command returns to the currently active form

Description
Use the Me command to write code that will work independently of the form on which it is executed.

AVAILABLE IN VB SCRIPT

Syntax
```
Me
```

Parameters
N/A

Returns
N/A

Immediate Window Sample
```
Me.Hide
```

SEE ALSO   Load, Show, Hide

Mid, Mid$

Returns a substring of the passed string of specified length and start position

Description

This function allows access to an exact substring within a string. The start argument determines where the desired string should begin. The lowest character position is 1. The length, if omitted, will be automatically set to the remaining length of the string.

The Mid, Mid$ functions can also have a different usage; see next function definition.

AVAILABLE IN VB SCRIPT

Syntax

```
Mid$(stringExpression$, start&[, Length&])
Mid(stringExpression$, start&[, Length&])
```

Parameters

stringExpression$ Required. Any valid string.

start&   Required. Start position within stringExpression$. Must be equal to 1.

Length&   Optional. Length of substring to return.

Returns

String type

Immediate Window Sample

```
? Mid$("Hello",2)
? Mid$("Hello",2,3)
```

SEE ALSO   Left, Left$, Right, Right$, Len

Mid, Mid$

Replaces a substring of the passed string of specified length and start position

Description

This function allows replacement of a substring within a string. The start argument determines where the desired string should begin. The lowest character position is 1. The length, if omitted, will be automatically set to the remaining length of the string.

The Mid, Mid$ functions can also have a different usage; see the previous function definition.

AVAILABLE IN VB SCRIPT

Syntax

```
Mid$(result-string$, start&[, Length&]) =
stringExpression$ Mid(result-string$, start&[,
Length&])
= stringExpression$
```

Parameters

result-string$ Required. Any valid string.

start&   Required. Start position within stringExpression$. Must be equal to 1.

Length&   Optional. Length of substring to return.

stringExpression$ Required. Any valid string.

Returns

N/A

Immediate Window Sample

```
a$="My new world"
Mid$(a$,4,3) = "big"
? a$
```

SEE ALSO   Left, Left$, Right, Right$, Mid (previous definition), Mid$ (previous definition)

Minute

Returns the minute portion of the date and time passed to it

Description
The Minute function will return the minute portion of a Date type.
An integer between 0 and 59 is returned.

AVAILABLE IN VB SCRIPT

Syntax
```
Minute(dateVariant)
```

Parameters
dateVariant   Required. The date from which the minute value will
be extracted.

Returns
Integer type

Immediate Window Sample
```
? Minute(Now)
```

SEE ALSO   Now, TimeSerial, TimeValue, Hour, Second

MIRR

Returns the modified internal rate of return

Description
This function works similarly to the IRR( ) function. The finance and
reinvestment rate is supplied to complete the calculations.

NOT AVAILABLE IN VB SCRIPT

Syntax
```
MIRR(valuesArray(), financeInterestRate!,
reinvestmentInternalRate!)
```

Parameters

valuesArray   Required. An Array containing at least one positive (receipt) and one negative (payment) item.

financeInterestRate!   Required. The cost of accounting interest rate.

reinvestmentInternalRate!   Required. The capital gains interest received from cash reinvestment.

Returns

Double type

Immediate Window Sample

```
myArray = array(-50000,12000,15000,10000)
? MIRR(myArray)
```

SEE ALSO   FV, IPmt, IIR, DDB, NPer, NPV, Pmt, PPmt, PV, Rate, SLN, SYD

MkDir

Creates a new directory at specified path

Description

This command will create a single directory. The command requires all directories leading up to where the new one is created to already exist. If current path information is omitted, the directory will be created in the default path.

NOT AVAILABLE IN VB SCRIPT

Syntax

```
MkDir dirname$
```

Parameters

dirname$ Any valid path string

Returns

N/A

Immediate Window Sample

MkDir "C:\vbtemp"

SEE ALSO   ChDrive, ChDir, RmDir, FileCopy, Open, Kill, Environ, CurDir

---

Mod

Modulo arithmetic operator

Description

The Mod operator allows you to obtain the remainder if the divisor doesn't divide evenly.

AVAILABLE IN VB SCRIPT

Syntax

B Mod C

Parameters

B, C   Any numeric expressions

Returns

Integer type

Immediate Window Sample

```
? 9 Mod 5
? 9 Mod 2
? 9 Mod 3
```

User Tip

This operator is perfect for finding a row number within a greater set. If a record in a sheet is seven rows long, using the Mod operator can instantly tell the row within the sheet as follows: ? ActiveCell.Row Mod 7.

SEE ALSO   Int, CInt, \, /

Month

2

Returns the Month portion of the passed Date type

Description
This function will return an integer value between 1 and 12 that represents the month of the date passed to it.

AVAILABLE IN VB SCRIPT

Syntax
Month(dateVariant)

Parameters
dateVariant   A valid date from which the Month will be extracted

Returns
Integer type

Immediate Window Sample
? Month(Now)

SEE ALSO   DateSerial, DateValue, Now, Day, IsDate, WeekDay, DateAdd, DateDiff, CVDate, Year

MsgBox

Displays a dialog box presenting information and possibly retrieving a user selection

Description
The message box is one of the most useful functions in the Visual Basic language, because it can quickly present information to the user or retrieve simple information without requiring the construction of a complete form. Since the MsgBox command can be used as either a function or a statement, the Immediate window example shows many of the ways it can be called.

Box types are numbers that represent the types of buttons shown, the icons displayed, and the modal setting. The buttons can include the OK button (0); the OK and Cancel buttons (1); the Abort, Retry, and Ignore buttons (2); the YesNoCancel buttons (3); the Yes and No buttons (4); or the Retry and Cancel buttons (5).

Icons include the Critical (16), the Question (32), the Exclamation (48), and the Information (64) icons. Including a SystemModel setting (4096) suspends all applications until the user dismisses the message box. Returned values include OK (1), Cancel (2), Abort (3), Retry (4), Ignore (5), Yes (6), and No (7).

AVAILABLE IN VB SCRIPT

Syntax
```
MsgBox(message$[, boxtype%][, windowtitle$])
```

Parameters
message$ Required. A String containing the message to be displayed.

boxtype%   Optional. The compilation of all the box type numbers to display the desired buttons, icons, and dialog type.

windowtitle$ Optional. Title of the message box.

Returns
Integer type

Immediate Window Sample
```
MsgBox "Hello World"
Call MsgBox("Hello World")
a = MsgBox("Hello World")
a = MsgBox("What should I do?",2+16+4096,"Proceed?")
```

SEE ALSO   InputBox, InputBox$

Name

Renames a file, directory, or folder

Description

The new path name and old path name must match except for the final change value. You cannot change the name of an open file.

NOT AVAILABLE IN VB SCRIPT

Syntax

`Name oldname As newname`

Parameters

oldname, newname   Required. Oldname must be a valid path or file.

Returns

N/A

Immediate Window Sample

`Name "test.txt" as "test2.txt"`

SEE ALSO   Kill, ChDir, Environ, Open, CurDir, ChDir, ChDrive

---

Not

Logical negation

Description

Using the Not operator on a number will actually create its bitwise negative, but this is not the same as a true negative. Try using the Not in the Immediate window to demonstrate this yourself.

AVAILABLE IN VB SCRIPT

Syntax

`Not expression`

Parameters

expression   A valid mathematical expression

Returns

Variant

Immediate Window Sample

```
? Not True
? Not 2=2
? Not 10
```

SEE ALSO And, Or, Xor, Exp

Now

Returns the current system date and time

Description

This function will return a Date type value containing the current date and time of the system.

AVAILABLE IN VB SCRIPT

Syntax

Now

Parameters

N/A

Returns

Variant type

Immediate Window Sample

```
? Now
```

SEE ALSO Day, Hour, Minute, Month, Second, WeekDay, Year, IsDate, Time, Timer, TimeValue, TimeSerial, DateSerial, DateAdd, DateDiff, DateValue, Date, Time

NPer

Returns the number of periods in an annuity

Description

The returned value is based on periodic fixed payments and a fixed interest rate. The interestRate must specify the rate per period, such as 0.0821 per month. The periodicPayment specifies the size of payment made each period. The presentValue determines the value of a series of future receipts and payments.

The futureValue is the desired cash value you wish to have once all of the payments are complete. The whenDue parameter instructs the function to calculate whether the payments are due at the end of the period (0), the default, or at the beginning of the period (1).

NOT AVAILABLE IN VB SCRIPT

Syntax

```
NPer(interestRate!, periodicPayment@, presentValue@
[, futureValue@, whenDue%])
```

Parameters

interestRate!   Required. Interest rate for the calculations.

periodicPayment@   Required. Size of each payment.

presentValue@   Required. Current value of payments.

futureValue@   Optional. Final cash value desired.

whenDue%   Optional. End (0) or beginning (1) of payment period.

Returns

Double type

Immediate Window Sample

```
? NPer(.0821,400,2000)
```

SEE ALSO   FV, IPmt, IIR, MIRR, DDB, NPV, Pmt, PPmt, PV, Rate, SLN, SYD

NPV

Returns the Net Present Value based on payments, receipts, and discount rate

Description

This function determines the current value of the future series of investments. These include the cash flow values of payments (negatives) and receipts (positives). The discountRate is stated as a percentage over the life of the investment.

NOT AVAILABLE IN VB SCRIPT

Syntax

```
NPV(discountRate!, valuesArray())
```

Parameters

discountRate   The rate of interest expressed as a decimal (that is, 5 percent = .05).

valuesArray   Required. Array that must contain at least one payment and one receipt.

Returns

Double type

Immediate Window Sample

```
myArray = array(-50000,12000,15000,10000)
? NPV(.05, myArray)
```

SEE ALSO   FV, IPmt, IIR, MIRR, NPer, DDB, Pmt, PPmt, PV, Rate, SLN, SYD

Oct, Oct$

Converts a number to its octal equivalent

Description

This function will create a string containing the hexadecimal (base 16 number) from the passed value. Each value may contain the numbers 0–9 and the letters A–F.

AVAILABLE IN VB SCRIPT

Syntax

```
Oct$(numericExpression) Oct(numericExpression)
```

Parameters
numericExpression   Required. Any numeric expression.

Returns
String type

Immediate Window Sample
```
? Oct(7)
? Oct(8)
? Oct(63)
? Oct(64)
```

SEE ALSO   Hex, Hex$, Val

On Error...

Creates error-trapping routine and jumps to prespecified areas of code when an error occurs

Description
The On Error routine will seize control when an error occurs. If the On Error routine instructs, the GoTo command will jump to a specified error-handler or line number. The On Error Resume Next command will simply ignore the error and execute the instruction that follows it. The On Error GoTo 0 command will disable the current error handler in the procedure or function.

NOT AVAILABLE IN VB SCRIPT

Syntax
```
On Error GoTo error-handler
error-handler:
    [statements]
Resume [{[0] | Next | {line-number | line-label} }]
```

To cause the Err flag to be set:

```
On Error Resume Next
```

or

```
On Error GoTo O
```

Parameters

error-handler   Label to indicate location of the error handler

Returns
N/A

Immediate Window Sample
N/A

SEE ALSO   Err, Error, Error$, Resume

On...GoSub

Jumps to a subroutine of code within a procedure or function based on the value of a numeric index

Description
Using a numeric index, the On...GoSub will jump to the routine in the Go Sub list in the index slot specified. A GoSub allows execution to return to the originator, where the On...GoTo routine changes the execution path.

NOT AVAILABLE IN VB SCRIPT

Syntax
```
On numericExpression GoSub Line1[, Line 3][, line255]
```

Parameters
numericExpression   Required. Specifies the number in the list that follows to branch to.

Returns
N/A

Immediate Window Sample
N/A

SEE ALSO   On...GoTo, SelectCase

On...GoTo

Changes execution to a subroutine of code within a procedure or function based on the value of a numeric index

Description
By use of a numeric index, the On...GoTo will jump to the routine in the GoTo list in the index slot specified.

NOT AVAILABLE IN VB SCRIPT

Syntax
```
On NumericExpression GoTo Line1[, Line 2][, line 3][,
Line255]
```

Parameters
numericExpression   Required. Specifies the number in the list that follows to branch to.

Returns
N/A

Immediate Window Sample
N/A

SEE ALSO   On...GoSub, SelectCase

Open

Opens a file for reading or writing

Description
This command is used to open a file with particular access options. Files of types Sequential, Binary, and Random may be opened.

NOT AVAILABLE IN VB SCRIPT

Syntax
```
Open filename$ [for mode] [Access access] [locktype]
As [#]filenumber [Len=recordLength]
```

Parameters
filename$ Required. Any valid path and filename.

mode   May include Input, Output, Binary, Append, and Random.

access   May include Read, Write, or Read Write.

locktype   May include Shared, Lock Read, Lock Write, and Lock Read Write.

filenumber   Required. Any valid file number between 1 and 511 as long as it isn't already in use.

recordLength   Number of characters buffered (Sequential) or record length (Random).

Returns
N/A

Immediate Window Sample
```
Open "C:\test.txt" for Output as #1 : _
Print #1,"Hello";Spc(20);"Hello2" : Close #1
```

SEE ALSO   Close, FreeFile, Get, Input, Input$, Line Input #, Put, Write

Option Base

Sets the default lower bounds for arrays

Description
Using this command allows you to define, at a module level, the lower bounds for an array. The default is typically 0, and the Dim command can be used to set the lower bounds on individual arrays.

NOT AVAILABLE IN VB SCRIPT

Syntax
Option Base {0 | 1}

Parameters
{0 | 1}   A lower bound of 0 or 1.

Returns
N/A

Immediate Window Sample
N/A

SEE ALSO   Dim, Global, ReDim

Option Compare

Sets the default comparison method for strings

Description
When strings are being compared, they can be compared by use of the Binary method, which differentiates between case, foreign alphabets, and so on, and the Text method, which does not. The default is set to Binary mode.

AVAILABLE IN VB SCRIPT

Syntax
Option Compare (Binary | Text)

Parameters
(Binary | Text)   Required. Specifies the comparison method.

Returns
N/A

Immediate Window Sample
N/A

SEE ALSO   StrComp, Option Explicit

Option Explicit

Requires that all variables be explicitly defined

Description
The Option Explicit command will make any execution generate an error if a variable is not explicitly defined with a Dim command.

AVAILABLE IN VB SCRIPT

Syntax
```
Option Explicit
```

Parameters
N/A

Returns
N/A

Immediate Window Sample
N/A

User Tip
Although frequently annoying because of the strict definition requirements, this command can save you hours of debugging time. Variables are always defined, so misspellings or misreferences become much less frequent.

SEE ALSO Dim

Or

Logical Or

Description
The Or operator will perform a logical Or on two numbers, or will do a logical truth on two Boolean values.

AVAILABLE IN VB SCRIPT

Syntax
a Or b

Parameters
a, b   Required. Any valid numeric expressions.

Returns
Variant

Immediate Window Sample
? True or False
? True or True
? False or False
? 1=2 or 1=1

SEE ALSO   And, Imp, Eqv, Xor, True, False, Not

Partition

Returns a string denoting where the passed number occurs within the ranges

Description
This function calculates ranges and the particular range in which the specified number falls. The returned string describes the range in the format *start:end*.

AVAILABLE IN VB SCRIPT

Syntax
Partition(number&, startRange&, endRange&, interval&)

Parameters
number&   Required. Number that will be evaluated against the ranges.

startRange&   Required. Number. The number 0 is used as the beginning of the overall range.

endRange&   Required. Number. The startRange is used as the end of the overall range.

interval&   Required. Number. The number 1 is used as the interval spanned by each range.

Returns
String type

Immediate Window Sample
```
? Partition(20,0,400,30)
```

SEE ALSO   Instr$

Pmt

Returns a payment value for an annuity

Description
The payment is calculated from the values of periodic fixed payments and fixed interest rate. The interestRate is specified in a decimal percentage for each period.

NOT AVAILABLE IN VB SCRIPT

Syntax
```
Pmt(interestRate!, numberOfPayments%, presentValue@
[, futureValue@, whenDue%])
```

Parameters
interestRate!   Required. Interest rate for the calculations.

numberOfPayments%   Required. Total number of payments.

presentValue@   Required. Current value of payments.

futureValue@   Optional. Final cash value desired.

whenDue%   Optional. End (0) or beginning (1) of payment period.

Returns
Double type

Immediate Window Sample

```
? Pmt(.0081,48,10000)
```

SEE ALSO   FV, IPmt, IIR, MIRR, NPer, NPV, DDB, PPmt, PV, Rate, SLN, SYD

PPmt

Returns the principal payment value for an annuity

Description

This function calculates the principal payment based on periodic payments and a fixed interest rate.

NOT AVAILABLE IN VB SCRIPT

Syntax

```
PPmt(interestRate!, whichPeriod%, totalPeriods%,
presentValue@[, FutureValue@, whenDue%])
```

Parameters

interestRate!   Required. Interest rate for the calculations.

whichPeriod%   Required. Total number of payments.

totalPeriods%   Required.

presentValue@   Required. Current value of payments.

futureValue@   Optional. Final cash value desired.

whenDue%   Optional. End (0) or beginning (1) of payment period.

Returns

Double type

Immediate Window Sample

```
? PPmt(.0081,12,48,10000)
```

SEE ALSO   FV, IPmt, IIR, MIRR, NPer, NPV, Pmt, DDB, PV, Rate, SLN, SYD

Print

Writes data to a specified Sequential file

Description
The Print # statement outputs variables or formatted text to the file denoted by the file number.

NOT AVAILABLE IN VB SCRIPT

Syntax
```
Print #filenumber, [[{Spc(n)|Tab(m)}]expres-
sion[{;|,}]...]
```

Parameters
filenumber   Required. Any valid open file number.

outputlist   Required. Any number of items may be included in the output list, such as strings, spaces, tabs, or expressions.

Returns
N/A

Immediate Window Sample
```
Open "C:\test.txt" for Output as #1 : _
Print #1,"Hello";Spc(20);"Hello2" : Close #1
```

SEE ALSO   Input, Input #, Write #

Private

Makes the variable scope private to a particular form, module, or routine

Description
Use of the Private statement will limit the scope of the form, module, procedure, or function.

NOT AVAILABLE IN VB SCRIPT

Syntax
```
Private [Function|Sub|variablename]
```

2

Parameters
N/A

Returns
N/A

Immediate Window Sample
N/A

SEE ALSO   Public, Dim, Sub, Function, Property Get, Property Let, Property Set

---

Property Get

Declares a property retrieval routine

Description
Use of the Property Get/Set/Let statements allows the program to minimize the direct access to internally used properties. In object-oriented programming, using these statements is known as "information hiding." By creating an indirect method to access properties, internal changes do not effect programs that access properties. Also, bounds checking can be performed before changes are made to the properties.

NOT AVAILABLE IN VB SCRIPT

Syntax
```
[Public|Private] [Static] Property Get name
[(arglist)] [As type] [statements] [Exit Property]
End Property
```

Parameters
name   Required. Any valid name expression. Can be the same as Property Let and Property Set names.

arglist   Required. List of variables to be passed to the Get statement when it is called.

Returns
N/A

Immediate Window Sample
N/A

User Tip
If you are beginning to use object-oriented methods, such as information hiding, make sure you use this structure to optimize your solution.

SEE ALSO   Sub, Function, Property Let, Property Set

Property Let

Declares a property definition routine

Description
Use of the Property Get/Set/Let statements allows the program to minimize the direct access to internally used properties. In object-oriented programming, using these statements is known as "information hiding." By creating an indirect method to access properties, internal changes do not effect programs that access properties. Also, bounds checking can be performed before changes are made to the properties.

NOT AVAILABLE IN VB SCRIPT

Syntax
```
[Public|Private] [Static] Property Let name
[(arglist)] [As type] [statements] [Exit Property]
End Property
```

Parameters
name   Required. Any valid name expression. Can be the same as Property Get and Property Set names.

arglist   Required. List of variables to be passed to the Let statement when it is called.

Returns
N/A

Immediate Window Sample
N/A

User Tip
If you are beginning to use object-oriented methods, such as information hiding, make sure you use this structure to optimize your solution.

SEE ALSO   Sub, Function, Property Get, Property Set

Property Set

Declares a property reference routine

Description
Use of the Property Get/Set/Let statements allows the program to minimize the direct access to internally used properties. In object-oriented programming, using these statements is known as "information hiding." By creating an indirect method to access properties, internal changes do not effect programs that access properties. Also, bounds checking can be performed before changes are made to the properties.

NOT AVAILABLE IN VB SCRIPT

Syntax
```
[Public|Private] [Static] Property Set name
[(arglist,) reference] [statements] [Exit Property]
End Property
```

Parameters
name   Required. Any valid name expression. Can be the same as Property Let and Property Get names.

arglist Required. List of variables to be passed to the Set statement when it is called.

Returns
N/A

Immediate Window Sample
N/A

User Tip
If you are beginning to use object-oriented methods, such as information hiding, make sure you use this structure to optimize your solution.

SEE ALSO Sub, Function, Property Let, Property Get

Public

Makes the variable scope public for access outside a form or module

Description
Using the Public statement will increase the scope of the form, module, procedure, or function so that it may be accessed from another object. References to a Public member from an external object require the hosting object name to be referenced (that is, myPublicForm.myPublicSub).

NOT AVAILABLE IN VB SCRIPT

Syntax
```
Public [Function|Sub|variablename]
```

Parameters
N/A

Returns
N/A

Immediate Window Sample
N/A

SEE ALSO   Dim, Sub, Function, Property Get, Property Let, Property Set

Put

Writes a variable to a current file

Description
The Put command works very much like the Print # command, except it outputs the contents of a single variable and provides no automatic formatting to the output.

NOT AVAILABLE IN VB SCRIPT

Syntax
Put [#]filenumber%, [position&], variablename

Parameters
filenumber%   Required. Any valid open file number.

position&   Optional. Specifies record number in a Random file or byte number in a Binary file where writing should occur.

variablename   Required. A valid variable that will have its contents written to the file.

Returns
N/A

Immediate Window Sample
```
a$ = "Hello World"
Open "C:\test.txt" for Output as #1 :_
Put #1,a$ : Close #1
```

SEE ALSO   Get, LOF, Open, Type

PV

Returns the present value of an annuity

Description
The function calculates the present value based on periodic payments and a fixed interest rate.

NOT AVAILABLE IN VB SCRIPT

Syntax
```
PV(interestRate!, totalPeriods%, payment@[,future-
Value@,whenDue%])
```

Parameters
interestRate!   Required. Interest rate for the calculations.

totalPeriods%   Required.

payment@   The amount of payment to be made each period.

futureValue@   Optional. Final cash value desired.

whenDue%   Optional. End (0) or beginning (1) of payment period.

Returns
Double type

Immediate Window Sample
```
? PV(.0081,48,2000)
```

SEE ALSO   FV, IPmt, IIR, MIRR, NPer, NPV, Pmt, PPmt, DDB, Rate, SLN, SYD

QBColor

Returns a standard Long color value from a QuickBasic color

Description

This command provides quick access to simple colors that are supported in the QuickBasic system included with most versions of Windows 3.1. QuickBasic color values include black (0), blue (1), green (2), cyan (3), red (4), magenta (5), yellow (6), white (7), gray (8), light blue (9), light green (10), light cyan (11), light red (12), light magenta (13), light yellow (14), and bright white (15).

NOT AVAILABLE IN VB SCRIPT

Syntax

QBColor(color-number%)

Parameters

color-number%   Required. A number between 0 and 15.

Returns

Long value

Immediate Window Sample

? QBColor(7)

User Tip

QBColor is excellent for quick color setting when you don't know exact RGB values of a particular shade. By simply using a single constant, you can use this function to retrieve the RGB long value.

SEE ALSO   RGB, Line

Randomize

Initializes the seed of the random generator

Description

This statement sets the random seed to a new number. Call this function before the first call to the Rnd( ) function to have a fairly random outcome.

AVAILABLE IN VB SCRIPT

Syntax
```
Randomize [seed]
```

Parameters
seed   Optional. Any valid numeric expression. If seed is omitted, the system timer is used for the seed.

Returns
N/A

Immediate Window Sample
```
Randomize
? Rnd
```

User Tip
To create an identical random sequence as earlier, call the Rnd( ) function with a negative value and then call Randomize with a numeric argument. Calling Randomize with the same number as previously used does not create the same sequence.

Many programmers mistakenly think the Rnd() function is a number rounding function. For rounding, see the Int, Fix, Format, and CInt functions.

SEE ALSO   Rnd, Timer

Rate

Returns the interest rate per period calculated from an annuity

Description
The payment is calculated from the values of periodic fixed payments and a fixed interest rate. The Rate returns the interest rate per period given the other factors.

NOT AVAILABLE IN VB SCRIPT

Syntax

```
Rate(totalPeriods%,payment@,presentValue@
[,futureValue@, whenDue%,guess!])
```

Parameters

totalPeriods%   Required.

payment@   The amount of payment to be made each period.

presentValue@   Required. Current value of payments.

futureValue@   Optional. Final cash value desired.

whenDue%   Optional. End (0) or beginning (1) of payment period.

guess!   Optional. Your estimate of the rate. If omitted, guess is set to 0.1 (10 percent).

Returns

Double type

Immediate Window Sample

```
? Rate(24,2000,12000)
```

SEE ALSO   FV, IPmt, IIR, MIRR, NPer, NPV, Pmt, PPmt, PV, DDB, SLN, SYD

ReDim

Redimensions an array size that can leave the data within the array intact

Description

This command can be used to resize an array. If the array is made bigger, the new array items are left blank. If smaller, the array is truncated and values outside the new array size are lost.

AVAILABLE IN VB SCRIPT

Syntax
```
ReDim [Preserve] name[subscript-range)][As type]
[, name{subscript-range){As type]]...
```

Parameters
Preserve   Optional. Preserve the data that exists with the array.

Returns
N/A

Immediate Window Sample
N/A

SEE ALSO   Dim, Erase, Global, Option Base

Rem

Makes any text following it on the current line invisible to the compiler

Description
The remark command can be used anywhere on a code line. Any text that follows it until the end of the line will be ignored.

AVAILABLE IN VB SCRIPT

Syntax
```
Rem comment
' comment
```

Parameters
comment   Optional. Any text.

Returns
N/A

Immediate Window Sample
N/A

User Tip
The remark command is very useful when you're testing code. Rather than delete the code, which you may need later, simply make it a comment.

SEE ALSO   ' (apostrophe)

2

Reset

Closes all open files

Description
Any files that were opened using the Open command will be closed and their file buffers written to disk. This works in the same manner as the Close command when Close is not passed any parameters.

NOT AVAILABLE IN VB SCRIPT

Syntax
Reset

Parameters
N/A

Returns
N/A

Immediate Window Sample
N/A

SEE ALSO   Open, Close, End, FreeFile, ChDir, ChDrive

Resume

Resumes execution after an error-handling routine has completed processing

Description

The Resume command can resume to the beginning of the procedure (Resume 0), with the next available statement (Resume Next), or with a particular anchor line or label.

AVAILABLE IN VB SCRIPT

Syntax

```
Resume [{[0] | Next | {line-number | line-label} }]
```

Parameters

{line-number | line-label}   An anchor where execution is to resume

Returns

N/A

Immediate Window Sample

N/A

SEE ALSO   On Error...

Return

Returns for a GoSub call within a subroutine

Description

The Return command moves execution back to the original call of the subroutine by its line or label.

NOT AVAILABLE IN VB SCRIPT

Syntax

```
Return
```

Parameters

N/A

Returns

N/A

Immediate Window Sample

N/A

SEE ALSO   GoSub, On...GoSub

RGB

Returns a Long value representing the three RGB values passed to it

Description

This function converts a Red value, a Green value, and a Blue value into the Long format typically used by the Windows system for everything from drawing to window background colors.

AVAILABLE IN VB SCRIPT

Syntax

```
RGB(red%, green%, blue%)
```

Parameters

red%   Integer value between 0 and 255

green%   Integer value between 0 and 255

blue%   Integer value between 0 and 255

Returns

Long type

Immediate Window Sample

```
? RGB(0,255,0)
```

SEE ALSO   QBColor, Line

Right, Right$

Returns a string containing the amount of the right portion of the passed string

Description
This function can be used to take any specified substring from the right to the left and to return it as a separate string.

AVAILABLE IN VB SCRIPT

Syntax
```
Right$(expression$, Length&)
```

Parameters
expression$ Any string expression

Length&   Number of characters to return in the substring

Returns
String type

Immediate Window Sample
```
? Right("Hello World",4)
```

User Tip
The Right$ function can be used to easily check a filename that the user entered to determine if he or she added the correct extension. For example, for a text file, the last four characters should equal .TXT.

SEE ALSO   Left, Left$, Mid, Mid$

RmDir

Removes the specified empty directory

Description

The directory to be removed must not contain any files. You can use the Kill command to delete the files before removing the directory.

NOT AVAILABLE IN VB SCRIPT

Syntax

```
RmDir dirname$
```

Parameters

dirname$ String must be in the format of
[*drive*:][\]*dir*[*subdir*][*subdir*]...

Returns

N/A

Immediate Window Sample

```
RmDir "c:\temp"
```

SEE ALSO   CurDir, CurDir$, MkDir, Kill

Rnd

Returns a random number

Description

This function returns a Single number between 0 and 1 that contains a seeded random number. You may include a specific seed for the random number. For random numbers within a range, use Int((ub-lb+1) * Rnd + lb), where lb = lower bound and ub = upper bound.

AVAILABLE IN VB SCRIPT

Syntax

```
Rnd[(numericExpression#)]
```

Parameters

numericExpression#   Any valid numeric expression

Returns
Single type

Immediate Window Sample
```
? Rnd
? Int((25-5+1)*Rnd+5)
```

User Tip
Many programmers mistakenly think the Rnd() function is a number rounding function. For rounding, see the Int, Fix, Format, and CInt functions.

SEE ALSO   Randomize

Rollback

Aborts operations currently in the transaction cycle

Description
When a transaction has begun with BeginTrans, Rollback will reverse all current operations within the transaction and abort it.

NOT AVAILABLE IN VB SCRIPT

Syntax
```
Rollback
```

Parameters
N/A

Returns
N/A

Immediate Window Sample
N/A

SEE ALSO   BeginTrans, CommitTrans

RSet

Right-justifies string within the destination and fills the remainder with spaces

Description

This command essentially copies the sourcevariable into the resultvariable, padded with spaces if the resultvariable is longer. For example, if the length of resultvariable is ten characters, a five-character sourcevariable would be copied to it and padded with five space characters. See this example in the Immediate window. This command can also be used to copy from one user-defined variable to another of the same length.

AVAILABLE IN VB SCRIPT

Syntax

```
RSet resultvariable = sourcevariable
```

Parameters

resultvariable   Required. Destination for the new string.

sourcevariable   Right-justified string to copy.

Returns

N/A

Immediate Window Sample

```
a$ = "1234567890"
RSet a$ = "Hello"
? a$ + "<-- end">
```

SEE ALSO   Let, LSet

RTrim, RTrim$

Returns a substring with the trailing spaces from the right removed from the passed string

Description

The RTrim function is the complement of the LTrim function, but returns a string taken from right to left. Any spaces on the right side of the string are removed.

AVAILABLE IN VB SCRIPT

Syntax

```
RTrim$(stringExpression$) RTrim(stringExpression$)
```

Parameters

stringExpression   Required. Any valid string.

Returns

String type

Immediate Window Sample

```
? RTrim("Hello ") + "<-end"
```

SEE ALSO   LTrim, LTrim$, Trim, Trim$

SavePicture

Saves the graphic stored in a Picture or Image control

Description

Not available in VBA. The SavePicture statement accepts the object reference to the picture, as well as a destination path and filename to store the file. SavePicture cannot save JPEG or GIF formats, so pictures in these formats are saved as bitmaps. Note that the Immediate window example requires that a form is executing but paused, and contains a Picture control named Picture1.

NOT AVAILABLE IN VB SCRIPT

Syntax

```
SavePicture objectReference, picturefile$
```

Parameters

objectReference   Required. The object reference stored in the Picture property of a control.

picturefile$ Required. A valid filename and path to store the picture.

Returns

N/A

Immediate Window Sample

```
SavePicture Picture1.Picture, "c:\myPict.bmp"
```

SEE ALSO   LoadPicture

Second

Returns the seconds portion of the date and time passed to it

Description

The Second function will return the seconds portion of a Date type. An integer between 0 and 59 is returned.

AVAILABLE IN VB SCRIPT

Syntax

```
Second(dateVariant)
```

Parameters

dateVariant   Required. The date from which the second value will be extracted.

Returns

Integer type

Immediate Window Sample

```
? Second(Now)
```

SEE ALSO   Now, TimeSerial, TimeValue, Hour, Minute, Time

Seek

Returns the current read/write position of an open file

Description
When passed a file number, this will return a Long value that varies depending on the type of file access. If the file is a Random file, the number of the next record is returned. If a Binary, Output, Append, or Input file is used, the byte position (beginning at byte 1) will be returned.

NOT AVAILABLE IN VB SCRIPT

Syntax
As a function:

```
Seek(filenumber%)
```

As a statement:

```
Seek [#]filenumber%, position&
```

Parameters
filenumber%   Required. Number of a currently open file.

Returns
Long

Immediate Window Sample
```
? Seek(#1)
```

SEE ALSO   Get, Open, Put, FileLen, Loc

Select Case

Executes a group of statements when an expression equals the testexpression

Description

The Select Case statement is an advanced form of an If...Then...Else structure, where one expression is entered and compared against multiple values. The Case Else statement allows statements to be executed if none of the values match.

AVAILABLE IN VB SCRIPT

Syntax

```
Select Case testexpression
   Case expression1
      [statements]
   [Case expression2]
      [statements]
   [Case Else]
      [statements]
End Select
```

Parameters

testexpression   Main value used for all comparisons

expression   Value to be compared with testexpression

Returns

N/A

Immediate Window Sample

```
a = 3
Select Case a : Case 1 : ? "1" : Case 2 : _
? "2" : Case Else : ? "Other" : End Select
```

SEE ALSO   If...Else, If...Else...End If, Iif, Choose Switch

SendKeys

Sends keystrokes to the active window

Description

This can be used to simulate keyboard entry and to access system functions such as Cut, Copy, and Paste not normally available to a Visual Basic program.

NOT AVAILABLE IN VB SCRIPT

Syntax

```
SendKeys keystrokes$[, wait%]
```

Parameters

keystrokes$ Required. String containing the keystrokes to be sent to the window.

wait%   Optional. If True, control is not returned to the program until keys have been processed. For immediate control to be returned, False (the default) may be used.

Returns

N/A

Immediate Window Sample

```
SendKeys "{ENTER}"
SendKeys "{F1}"
SendKeys "{PrtSc}"
```

SEE ALSO   DoEvents

Set

Creates a reference to an object

Description

The Set command does not create the object instance, but merely points the variable at the object. More than one reference to a particular object may exist. Use the New command to create a new instance of the object.

AVAILABLE IN VB SCRIPT

Syntax

```
Set objectVariableName = [New] objectExpression
Set objectVariableName = Nothing
```

Parameters

objectVariableName   Required. Name of the variable that will receive the object reference.

objectExpression   Required. Expression to create a new object or to reference an existing one.

Returns

N/A

Immediate Window Sample

```
Set a = GetObject("Excel.Application")
a.Visible = True
```

SEE ALSO   Let, GetObject, CreateObject, With...End With

SetAttr

Sets the attributes of a file given a proper filename and path

Description

SetAttr can set the information of files as Normal (0), ReadOnly (1), Hidden (2), System (4), Directory (16), or Archive (32) designations. These attributes can be set for any file on the disk. The Immediate window sample hides the **TEST.TXT** file.

NOT AVAILABLE IN VB SCRIPT

Syntax

```
SetAttr fileName$, attributeBits%
```

Parameters

fileName$ Required. A valid path and filename.

attributeBits%   Required. New attribute settings.

Returns

N/A

Immediate Window Sample

```
? SetAttr("c:\test.txt",2)
```

SEE ALSO   GetAttr

SetDataAccess

Sets the location of the current workgroup setting for a database

Description

This is used to set the location of the data access options. It is obsolete and only available for backwards compatibility.

NOT AVAILABLE IN VB SCRIPT

Syntax

```
SetDataAccessOption option%, value
```

Parameters

option%   Numeric option of data access type (1 = set the name and path of the application INI file)

value   Parameter for the specified option

Returns

N/A

Immediate Window Sample

N/A

SEE ALSO   SetDefaultWorkspace

SetDefaultWorkspace

Sets the default user name and password for accessing secure databases

Description

This command will set a default user name and password that will be automatically passed to the database when a secure database is opened. It is obsolete and only available for backwards compatibility.

NOT AVAILABLE IN VB SCRIPT

Syntax

```
SetDefaultWorkspace userName$, password$
```

Parameters

userName$ Valid user name

password$ Valid password

Returns

N/A

Immediate Window Sample

N/A

SEE ALSO   SetDataAccess

Sgn

Returns the sign (+/-) of the number passed to it

Description

The Sgn function can be used to determine the sign of a number. A positive number returns a 1, a negative number returns a −1. If the passed value is 0, a 0 is returned.

AVAILABLE IN VB SCRIPT

Syntax
```
Sgn(numericExpression)
```

Parameters
numericExpression   Required. Any valid numeric expression.

Returns
Integer type

Immediate Window Sample
```
? Sgn(5)
? Sgn(-5)
? Sgn(0)
```

SEE ALSO   Abs, Tan, Atn, Sin, Cos, Log, Exp

Shell

Executes a command at the command prompt

Description
Use of the Shell command gives complete access to all command-prompt (MS-DOS) functions. This command is most often used to launch another program. Using traditional command line parameters, this command can be used to pass information to the launching application including toggle commands or parameters.

A taskID is returned if the command is successful. The mode allows you to control the execution window so it's hidden (0), normal with focus (1), minimized with focus (2), maximized with focus (3), normal without focus (4), or minimized without focus (6).

NOT AVAILABLE IN VB SCRIPT

Syntax
```
Shell(program-name$[, mode%])
```

Parameters

program-name   Required. Fully qualified path and filename.

mode%   Optional. Specifies in what mode to execute the command.

Returns
Double type

Immediate Window Sample
```
Shell "c:\windows\calc.exe"
```

SEE ALSO   AppActivate

Show Method

Makes the current window visible

Description
This method can be used on a nonload form to load and display it. If the Form window was previously hidden or opened with the Load command, the Show method will make it visible.

AVAILABLE IN VB SCRIPT

Syntax
```
window.Show
```

Parameters
window   Required. The Name property of a window within the project.

Returns
N/A

Immediate Window Sample
N/A

SEE ALSO   Load, Unload

Sin

Returns the sine of an angle specified in radians

Description
This command requires the angle to be passed in radians. The formula radians = (degrees*pi)/180 can be used to determine the radians from a degree measure.

AVAILABLE IN VB SCRIPT

Syntax
Sin(angle)

Parameters
angle   Required. Any numeric expression holding a radian measure.

Returns
Double type

Immediate Window Sample
? sin(3.14159)
? sin((90*3.14159)/180)

SEE ALSO   Abs, Tan, Atn, Sgn, Cos, Log, Exp, Sqr

SLN

Returns the value for a single period of straight line depreciation

Description
Depreciation is determined by use of a double-declining balance method unless specified by use of the factor parameter.

NOT AVAILABLE IN VB SCRIPT

Syntax
SLN(initialCost@, salvageValue@, lifeSpan%)

Parameters

initialCost@ Required. Initial cost of asset as Double type.

salvageValue@ Required. Value at end of useful life as Double type.

lLifeSpan% Required. Length of useful life as Double type.

Returns

Double

Immediate Window Sample

```
? SLN(10000,500,24)
```

SEE ALSO FV, IPmt, IIR, MIRR, NPer, NPV, Pmt, PPmt, PV, Rate, DDB, SYD

Space, Space$

Returns a string containing the number of spaces specified

Description

This function can be used for formatting to pad any number of spaces required.

AVAILABLE IN VB SCRIPT

Syntax

```
Space$(number-of-spaces&)
Space(number-of-spaces&)
```

Parameters

number-of-spaces& Required. Numeric expression containing the number of spaces to create.

Returns

String type

Immediate Window Sample

```
? Space(10);"Hello"
```

SEE ALSO Spc, String, String$, Print, ?

Spc

Adds spaces for formatting specifically for Print and Print # commands

Description
The Spc function adds spaces to the current print position. If the number of spaces exceeds the line width, the spaces will be placed on the next line in the next print position.

NOT AVAILABLE IN VB SCRIPT

Syntax
```
Spc(number-of-spaces%)
```

Parameters
number-of-spaces%   Required. Numeric expression containing the number of spaces to create.

Returns
N/A

Immediate Window Sample
```
Open "C:\test.txt" for Output as #1 : _
Print #1,"Hello";Spc(20);"Hello2" : Close #1
```

SEE ALSO Space, Space$, Tab

Sqr

Returns the square root of a given number

Description
The square root function will return the square root of any number greater than or equal to zero.

AVAILABLE IN VB SCRIPT

Syntax
```
Sqr(numericExpression)
```

Parameters
numericExpression   Required. Any valid numeric expression.

Returns
Double type

Immediate Window Sample
```
? Sqr(9)
? Sqr(2)
```

SEE ALSO   Sin, Abs, Tan, Atn, Sgn, Cos, Log, Exp, Sqr

Static

Makes a variable persistent even after the procedure has completed executing

Description
The Static command will make a variable that is local to a particular routine keep its value. The next execution of the routine can access the remaining value.

AVAILABLE IN VB SCRIPT

Syntax
For declaring the data type of a simple variable:

```
Static name [As type][, name [As type]]...
```

For declaring an array:

```
Static name[(subscript-range)][As type]
[, name [(subscript-range)][As type] syntax as
type]...
```

Parameters

Standard variable definitions

Returns

N/A

Immediate Window Sample

N/A

SEE ALSO Dim, Global, Option Base, ReDim, Type

Stop

Halts execution of the program

Description

Placing a Stop command in your program essentially places a semi-permanent breakpoint so the debugger will be activated when the Stop is executed. Since breakpoints don't save with a file, the Stop command allows the creation of a breakpoint that will be stored in the program.

NOT AVAILABLE IN VB SCRIPT

Syntax

```
Stop
```

Parameters

N/A

Returns

N/A

Immediate Window Sample

N/A

SEE ALSO End

2

Str, Str$

Converts an expression to a string

Description
The Str function will return a string representation and only recognizes the period (.) as a decimal separator.

AVAILABLE IN VB SCRIPT

Syntax
`Str$(numericExpression)`

Parameters
numericExpression   Required. Any valid numeric expression.

Returns
String type

Immediate Window Sample
```
? Str$(5)
? Str$(5+10)
```

SEE ALSO   Val, Instr$, CStr, Format

StrComp

Compares two strings

Description
This function will compare two strings using a specified method and return a result of the comparison. The compareType can be a binary comparison (0, default), a textual comparison (1), or, for Microsoft Access, a comparison based on information in a database. The results returned by the comparison can indicate that string1 < string2 (−1), string1 = string2 (0), string1 > string2 (1), or string1 or string2 = Null (Null).

AVAILABLE IN VB SCRIPT

Syntax

```
StrComp(string1$, string2$ [, compareType%])
```

Parameters

string1$, string2$ Required. Any valid strings.

compareType%   Optional. Specifies comparison method.

Returns

Integer

Immediate Window Sample

```
? StrComp("Hello","hello")
? StrComp("Hello","hello",1)
? StrComp("Hello","jello",1)
```

SEE ALSO   Instr$, Option Compare, =

String, String$

Creates a repeating string of the specified character

Description

The function can be passed a length and a string or ASCII code that will be duplicated until the string length is reached.

AVAILABLE IN VB SCRIPT

Syntax

```
String$(number-of-characters&, ascii-code%)
String$(number-of-characters&, character$)
String(number-of-characters&, ascii-code%)
String(number-of-characters&, character$)
```

Parameters

number-of-characters&   Required. Length the returned string will be.

ascii-code%   The ASCII value of a character to be repeated to fill the string.

character$ A single character string to be repeated.

Returns
String type

Immediate Window Sample
```
? String$(20,65)
? String$(25,"B")
```

SEE ALSO   Space, Space$, Asc, Chr

Sub...End Sub

Creates a subroutine in a module or form

Description
This command allows definition of a subroutine that may include the types of arguments that will be received when the routine is called.

AVAILABLE IN VB SCRIPT

Syntax
```
[Static] [Private] Sub sub-name[(arguments)]
[Static var[,var]...] [Dim var[,var]...]
[ReDim var[,var]...] [statements] [Exit Static]
   [statements]
End Sub
```

Parameters
arguments   Required. Any arguments to be received by the function.

Returns
N/A

Immediate Window Sample
N/A

SEE ALSO   Call, End, Exit, Function

Switch

Evaluates the passed expressions and returns the expression for
the first true expression

Description
The Switch function can be used to do a quick series of related
comparisons. The Immediate window example demonstrates
converting from an abbreviation to a complete string.

AVAILABLE IN VB SCRIPT

Syntax
```
Switch(expression1, value [, expression2, value2 [,.
. . expression7, value7] )
```

Parameters
expression   Boolean. Can be an evaluative expression.

value   Any valid Variant type variable.

Returns
Variant type

Immediate Window Sample
```
a$ = "CA"
? Switch(a$="WI","Wisconsin",a$="OR","Oregon,_
a$="CA","California")
```

SEE ALSO   Choose, IIf, Select Case

Tab   **193**

SYD

2

Returns the sum depreciation of the years digits of an asset

Description
Depreciation is determined by use of a double-declining balance method unless specified by use of the factor parameter.

AVAILABLE IN VB SCRIPT

Syntax
```
SYD(initialCost@, salvageValue@, Lifespan%, period%)
```

Parameters
initialCost@   Required. Initial cost of asset as Double type.

salvageValue@   Required. Value at end of useful life as Double type.

Lifespan%   Required. Length of useful life as Double type.

period%   Required. Period for which depreciation is calculated as Double type.

Returns
Double type

Immediate Window Sample
```
? SYD(10000,500,24,12)
```

SEE ALSO   DDB, FV, IPmt, IIR, MIRR, NPer, NPV, Pmt, PPmt, PV, Rate, SLN

Tab

Adds a tab to the formatting for a Print or Print # statement

Description

Tab can be used to properly format columns for output to files. If the position specified in the column has already passed, the characters will automatically be aligned with the next column position.

AVAILABLE IN VB SCRIPT

Syntax

```
Tab([column%])
```

Parameters

column%   Optional. Integer that specifies the column to tab into.

Returns

N/A

Immediate Window Sample

```
? Tab + "Hello"
? Tab(5) + "Hello"
```

SEE ALSO   Print #, Spc, Print, ?

Tan

Returns the tangent of an angle specified in radians

Description

This command requires the angle to be passed in radians. The formula radians = (degrees*pi)/180 can be used to determine the radians from a degree measure.

AVAILABLE IN VB SCRIPT

Syntax

```
Tan(angle)
```

Parameters

angle   Required. Any numeric expression holding a radian measure.

Returns

Double type

Immediate Window Sample

```
? tan(3.14159)
? tan((90*3.14159)/180)
```

SEE ALSO   Atn, Cos, Sin, Sqr

Time

Sets the current system time

Description

This function sets the actual system time, so be careful with its use.

AVAILABLE IN VB SCRIPT

Syntax

```
Time = time-string$
```

Parameters

time-string$ Required. String containing a valid time setting.

Returns

N/A

Immediate Window Sample

```
Time = "2:40"
? Time
```

SEE ALSO   Time$, Date$, Date, Now

Time$

Retrieves the time from the current system

Description
This returns a string that contains the current system time.

AVAILABLE IN VB SCRIPT

Syntax
Time$

Parameters
N/A

Returns
String type

Immediate Window Sample
? Time$

SEE ALSO   Date, Date$, Now, TimeValue

Timer

Returns the number of seconds that have elapsed since midnight

Description
This function, available in both VBA and VB Script, where there are no Timer controls available, can be used to track time values.

AVAILABLE IN VB SCRIPT

Syntax
Timer

Parameters
N/A

Returns
Single type

Immediate Window Sample
```
? Timer
a = Timer
? Timer - a
```

User Tip
To time the speed of programs, the Timer function can be very useful. Simply set a variable equal to the current timer (that is, a=Timer), execute the routine, and then figure the time elapsed (that is, myTime=Timer–a)).

SEE ALSO   Randomize

TimeSerial

Returns a time based on serial parameters passed to it

Description
This routine allows the quick creation of a date from three integer values.

AVAILABLE IN VB SCRIPT

Syntax
```
TimeSerial(hour%, minute%, second%)
```

Parameters
hour%, **minute%**, **second%**   Required. Integers.

Returns
Variant (Date) type

Immediate Window Sample
```
? TimeSerial(14,34,15)
```

SEE ALSO   DateSerial, TimeValue, DateValue, Day, Month, Now, Year, Date, Time, Format, CVDate

TimeValue

Creates a Date type value holding the specified time

Description
This function can be used to create a date and time value from a string containing a time string.

AVAILABLE IN VB SCRIPT

Syntax
```
TimeValue(time-string$)
```

Parameters
time-string$ Required. Any valid string holding a time value.

Returns
Variant (Date) type

Immediate Window Sample
```
? TimeValue("2:15:23 PM")
```

SEE ALSO   Now, TimeSerial

Trim, Trim$

Returns a string with both leading and trailing spaces removed

Description
Just as the LTrim command removes leading space and the RTrim removes trailing spaces, Trim removes both.

AVAILABLE IN VB SCRIPT

Syntax
```
Trim$(stringExpression$) Trim(stringExpression)
```

Parameters

stringExpression   Required. Any valid string.

Returns

String type

Immediate Window Sample

```
? Trim(" Hello ")
```

SEE ALSO   LTrim, LTrim$, RTrim, RTrim$

True

Logical True

Description

This constant can be used in most expressions, bitwise operations, and comparisons.

AVAILABLE IN VB SCRIPT

Syntax

```
True
```

Parameters

N/A

Returns

N/A

Immediate Window Sample

```
? (2=2) = False
? (2=2) = True
```

SEE ALSO   And, Or, Imp, Eqv, Xor, False

Type...End Type

Creates a user-defined variable type

Description
User-defined types are ideal when you need to format a set of information into a single structure such as rectangle data, data records, and so on.

NOT AVAILABLE IN VB SCRIPT

Syntax
```
Type type-name element As type [element As type] : :
End Type
```

Parameters
type-name   Required. Any valid name.

element   Required. The name of the structure member.

type   Required. Any valid data type.

Returns
N/A

Immediate Window Sample
N/A

User Tip
You can easily create your own type for storage of a rectangle. It might look like this: Type myRect top As Integer left As Integer width As Integer height As Integer End Type

SEE ALSO   Dim, Global, ReDim, Static

UBound

Returns the highest subscript available in the array

Description

This function can be used to determine the upper bound of an array. If the array is multidimensional, use the dimension argument to specify the upper bound to be returned.

NOT AVAILABLE IN VB SCRIPT

Syntax

```
UBound(arrayname[, dimension%])
```

Parameters

arrayname   Required. The name of the array required to determine the limit.

dimension%   Optional. The subscript dimension of a multidimensional array.

Returns

Long type

Immediate Window Sample

```
myArray = array(6,4,2,5,2,4,6)
? UBound(myArray)
```

SEE ALSO   Lbound, Array, Dim

UCase, UCase$

Returns a completely uppercase string

Description

This function converts all of the characters in the passed string to uppercase.

AVAILABLE IN VB SCRIPT

Syntax

```
UCase$(expression$)
UCase(expression$)
```

Parameters

expression$ Required. Any valid string.

Returns

String type

Immediate Window Sample

```
? UCase("hElLo")
```

SEE ALSO LCase, LCase$

Unload

Unloads a form or control object from memory

Description

Use the Unload command to release a control or form. Memory
used by the form or control will be flushed, and any property
setting will be lost.

NOT AVAILABLE IN VB SCRIPT

Syntax

```
UnLoad form-name
UnLoad control-name (index)
```

Parameters

form-name, **control-name** Required. Name to reference desired
object.

Returns

N/A

Immediate Window Sample

N/A

SEE ALSO Load, Show

Val

Returns the value contained in a string

Description

This function will convert the value contained within a string to a numeric value. If there is no numeric value contained in the string, a zero will be returned.

AVAILABLE IN VB SCRIPT

Syntax

```
Val(stringExpression$)
```

Parameters

stringExpression$ Required. Any string containing a numeric value.

Returns

Variant

Immediate Window Sample

```
? Val("100")
? Val("54.55")
```

SEE ALSO   Str, Str$, Format, &

Value Property

Holds the value for a specific control property

Description

The Value property is the most common property available for objects. It typically holds the central data for the control. For example, in a scroll bar control, the Value property holds the current thumb position.

AVAILABLE IN VB SCRIPT

Syntax
object.Value [= value]

Parameters
value   Dependent on the object type

Returns
N/A

Immediate Window Sample
? myScroll1.Value

SEE ALSO   . (dot)

VarType

Returns the type of variable stored in the passed reference

Description
Since Visual Basic variables may be defined implicitly, this function can be used to determine the type of variable being used. The returned type number may indicate Empty (0), Null (1), Integer (2), Long (3), Single (4), Double (5), Currency (6), Date (7), String (8), Object (9), Error (10), Boolean (11), Variant (12), Dataobject (13), Decimal (14), Byte (17), or Array (8192).

AVAILABLE IN VB SCRIPT

Syntax
Vartype(variant)

Parameters
variant   Required. A value to be evaluated.

Returns
Integer type

Immediate Window Sample

```
a$ = "Hello"
? VarType(a)
b% = 15
? VarType(b)
```

SEE ALSO   Dim, CInt, CStr, CDbl, CByte

WeekDay

Returns the weekday portion of the passed Date type

Description

This function will return an Integer value between 1 (Sunday) and 7 (Saturday) that represents the weekday of the date passed to it.

AVAILABLE IN VB SCRIPT

Syntax

```
WeekDay(dateVariant)
```

Parameters

dateVariant   A valid date from which the weekday will be extracted

Returns

Integer type

Immediate Window Sample

```
? WeekDay(Now)
```

SEE ALSO   DateSerial, DateValue, Day, Month, Year, Now, Format

While...Wend

Cycles through a loop until the necessary condition is met

Description

The While...Wend structure can continue cycling while a condition is True. It is recommended that you use the Do...Loop structure.

AVAILABLE IN VB SCRIPT

Syntax

```
While condition : [statements} : Wend
```

Parameters

condition   Required. Boolean value.

Returns

N/A

Immediate Window Sample

```
i=0
While i<5 :? i : i = i + 1 : Wend
```

SEE ALSO   Do...Loop, For...Next, For Each

Width

Sets a width for the output file

Description

For formatting to a file, the Width # statement will set the width between 0 and 255 for text, tabs, and spaces to be formatted. If the width is set to 0 (default), there is no set line width.

AVAILABLE IN VB SCRIPT

Syntax

```
Width #filenumber, width%
```

Parameters

filenumber   Required. Any valid open file number.

width%   Required. Any width between 0 and 255.

Returns
N/A

Immediate Window Sample
```
Open "C:\test.txt" for Output as #1 : Width #1,20 : _
Print #1,"Hello";Spc(15);"Hello2" : Close #1
```

SEE ALSO   Print #, Spc, Tab

With...End With

Used for a series of object references

Description
The With...End With structure allows any statement contained
within it to reference the current object with a simple dot (.)
command. For example, the Value property of a cell may be set
inside a With operator with the ".Value = 3" command.

AVAILABLE IN VB SCRIPT

Syntax
```
With object [statements] End With
```

Parameters
object   Required. Any valid object reference.

Returns
N/A

Immediate Window Sample
N/A

User Tip
Use the With...End With structure when you want to increase the
speed of your object references. When an object is accessed
multiple times and is several dot (.) levels deep, use of a width to
create a single reference is much faster.

SEE ALSO   CreateObject, GetObject

Write

Writes data to a specified open file

Description
Unlike the Print # command, Write # can write any type of data to a file without conversion into a string.

NOT AVAILABLE IN VB SCRIPT

Syntax
```
Write #filenumber[, var1][, var2][, var3]...
```

Parameters
filenumber   Required. Any valid open file number.

var   Optional. Variables of any valid type.

Returns
N/A

Immediate Window Sample
```
Open "C:\test.txt" for Output as #1 :_
Print #1, "Hello";Spc(20);"Hello2" : Close #1
```

SEE ALSO   Open, Print #, Write, Close, Input #

Xor

Exclusive Or

Description
This can be used to logically combine two numbers.

AVAILABLE IN VB SCRIPT

Syntax
```
a Xor b
```

Parameters
a, **b**   Required. Any valid numeric expression.

Returns
Variant

Immediate Window Sample
```
? 255 Xor 8
```

SEE ALSO   And, Or, Imp, Eqv, True, False, Not

Year

Returns the Year portion of the passed Date type

Description
This function will return a Variant value between 0 and 9999 that represents the year of the date passed to it.

AVAILABLE IN VB SCRIPT

Syntax
```
Year(dateVariant)
```

Parameters
dateVariant   A valid date from which the Year will be extracted

Returns
Variant

Immediate Window Sample
```
? Year(Now)
```

SEE ALSO   DateSerial, DateValue, Now, WeekDay, Month, Day

Part III
Object Model Diagrams

Programming VBA requires understanding many different facets of the programming world. Increasingly, programmers have divided large programs into a series of objects that work together. Most programs that incorporate the VBA language and development system are constructed of objects that are individually accessible. Knowing the object model (represented by an object diagram), a designer can create programs that can accomplish almost any operation available to the hands-on user. Spreadsheets can be added, text inserted into Word documents, contacts sorted in Outlook, and most other capabilities.

Part III of this reference provides the complete object models of all of the central Office applications as well as several other popular models. For the primary Office applications and Internet Explorer, the most common object methods and properties are provided, as well as a general explanation of the object model itself. The Immediate window provides an easy way to test and understand how an object, method, or property can be used. Therefore, where possible, single-line Immediate window samples have been provided.

For Outlook and Internet Explorer, there is no Immediate window available. Therefore, the Outlook code can be placed in the Scripting window and executed from there. Internet Explorer samples have been included as simple HTML files that can be created in any text editor (such as Notepad) and saved to the disk. Internet Explorer can then be used to open the example from a file using the Browse button under the Open option.

The object model diagrams have the complete set of objects available to each application. Multiple objects are stored as a *collection*. A collection is typically named as a plural of an object. On the diagrams, each collection appears as a set of stacked cards, while the individual objects appear as single boxes. In a collection box, the collection is named first, followed by the name of the individual objects in parentheses.

The most effective way to program the object models is to use them in conjunction with the Object Browser (pressing the F2 key will show the browser in the VBA environment) that is included

211

with all of the VB and VBA environments (it isn't included with Outlook or Internet Explorer). Use the object models to determine which objects you will need to access, and then look up the individual properties and methods within the Object Browser. Although the Object Browser itself is not available in Outlook and Internet Explorer, their object models are available for browsing through the Object Browser by using it from another Office application.

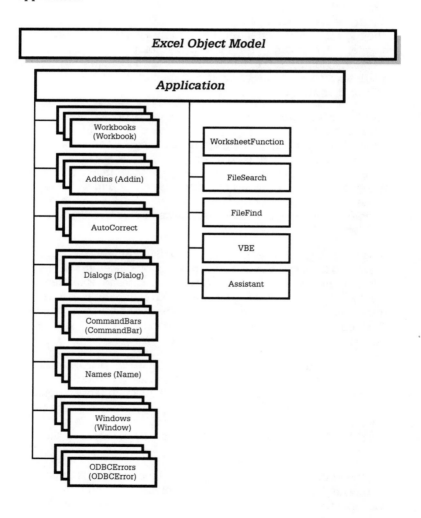

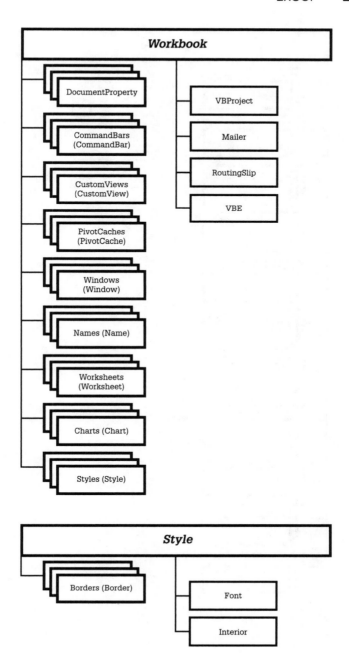

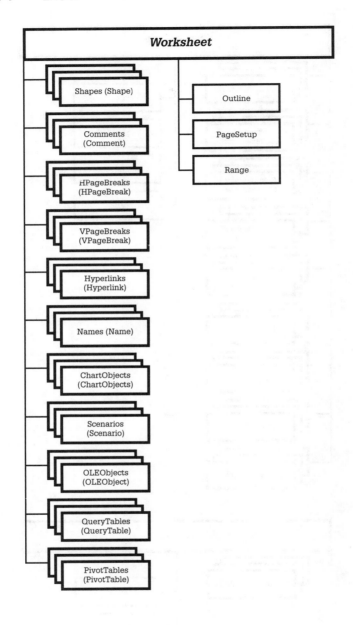

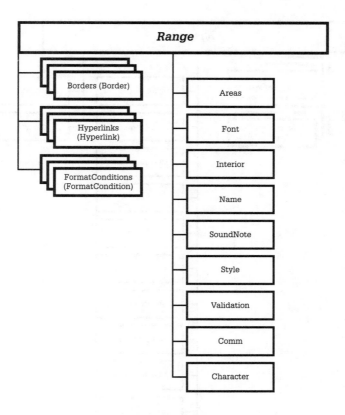

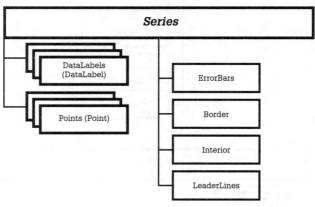

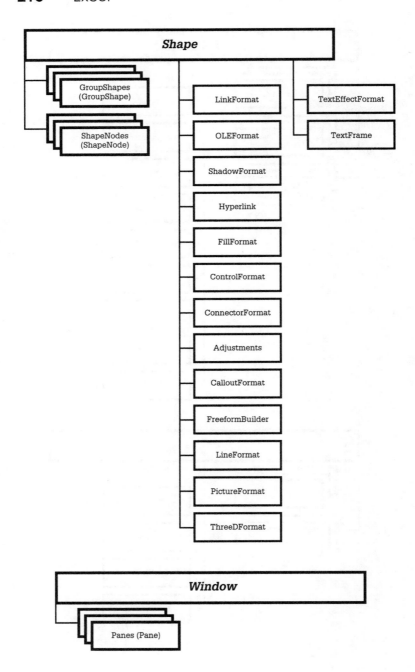

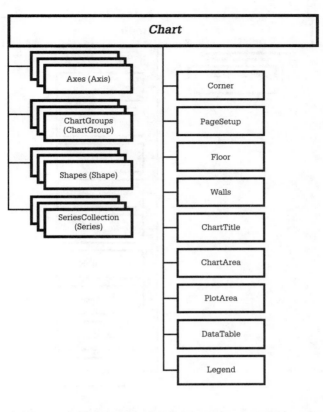

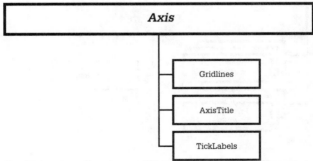

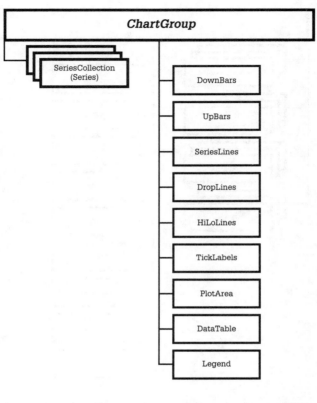

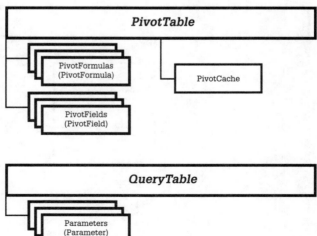

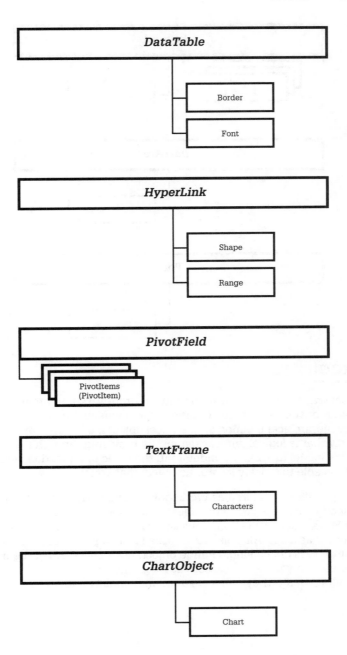

3

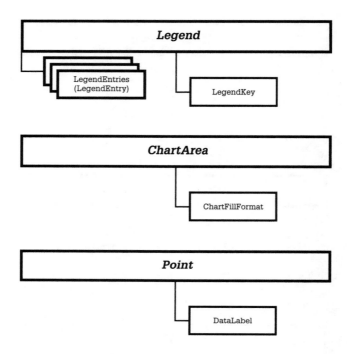

Excel

Excel was the first application to incorporate VBA and provides the
most robust object implementation. Spreadsheets break down in a
very hierarchical manner, so the Excel object model will appear in
a way that is logical and consistent. By browsing through the
object model diagram to understand the basic organization, you
will be able to quickly locate the object that you need.

All open files are stored as Workbook objects in the Workbooks
collection. In turn, each Worksheet in a Workbook is stored within
the Worksheets collection. Cells can be accessed individually or
selected as a set. All cells are accessed from a Range object. Note
that there is only a single Range object, not a collection of them.
Therefore if you need to access several different ranges
simultaneously, they will have to be individually stored.

Activate Method

Activates the current specified object

Description

The Activate method can be used to activate a Workbook, Worksheet, Chart, Window, Pane, Range, or OLE object. It functions essentially like the Select method for Workbook, Worksheet, Chart, Range, and OLE objects. To activate a single cell (with the Range object), it is recommended you use this method over Select.

AVAILABLE IN VB SCRIPT

Syntax

```
[object.] Activate
```

Parameters

N/A

Returns

N/A

Immediate Window Sample

```
Sheets("Sheet2").Activate
```

SEE ALSO   ActiveSheet, ActiveWorkbook, Select

ActiveCell Property

Returns an object reference to the current active cell of the active sheet of the active workbook

Description

The ActiveCell property can be used to quickly set or determine information about the current cell. The value contained within a cell, the formula, and the formatting are all obtainable through this property.

Syntax

```
[Application.] ActiveCell
```

Parameters

N/A

Returns

Variant type

Immediate Window Sample

```
? ActiveCell.Value
```

SEE ALSO   ActiveSheet, ActiveWorkbook

ActiveSheet Property

Returns an object reference to the current active sheet of the active workbook

Description

This property gives instant access to the currently selected sheet. It is especially useful when a button or macro is created to modify any sheet the user currently has selected. If no sheet is selected, access through the ActiveSheet object will generate an error.

AVAILABLE IN VB SCRIPT

Syntax

```
[Application.] ActiveSheet
```

Parameters

N/A

Returns

N/A

Immediate Window Sample

`? ActiveSheet.Name`

SEE ALSO   ActiveCell, ActiveWorkbook

ActiveWorkbook Property

Returns an object reference to the current active workbook

Description

This property gives instant access to the current workbook.

AVAILABLE IN VB SCRIPT

Syntax

`[Application.] ActiveWorkbook`

Parameters

N/A

Returns

N/A

Immediate Window Sample

`? ActiveWorkbook.Name`

SEE ALSO   ActiveSheet, ActiveCell

Add Method

Used to add worksheets, workbooks, and so on

Description

Use this method to add an object to the current object collection. The Immediate window example displays adding a Workbook object to the current Excel workspace and a worksheet to the current Workbook. The Add method creates instances of these objects in memory, but doesn't automatically save them. When creating an automated solution, make sure to save or close the documents you've added or modified, otherwise the program will stop execution and wait for a dialog asking for saving information that will be transparent to the user.

AVAILABLE IN VB SCRIPT

Syntax
```
Set myObject = object.Add
```

Parameters
N/A

Returns
Object type

Immediate Window Sample
```
Application.Workbooks.Add
Set a = ActiveWorkbook.Sheets.Add
```

SEE ALSO   ActiveSheet, ActiveWorkbook, DisplayAlerts

AutoFilter Method

Toggles the AutoFilter setting to place the current sheet or selection in Filter mode

Description
Using the AutoFilter from a VBA program can be the quickest way to do multivariable queries. The AutoFilter may be used to select columns of information that match specific criteria. The rows that match this criteria can be copied to the Clipboard and pasted into another sheet. Use the Macro Recorder to understand how this works.

Note that one of the idiosyncrasies of the AutoFilter is the first row inclusion. If the first physical row in the sheet matches the criteria, it becomes the first logical row in the AutoFilter. However, if the first physical row does not match, the second logical row on the sheet begins the set that matches the criteria. If your program uses the AutoFilter, be sure to manually check the first row to determine where to begin copying.

AVAILABLE IN VB SCRIPT

Syntax
```
range.AutoFilter([[[[Field], Criteria1], Operator], Criteria2])
```

3

Parameters
range   Range object to begin AutoFilter.

Field   Field # to conduct filter.

Criteria1, Criteria2   Values to match for the filter.

Operator   Optional. Can be set to determine how filtered results are displayed. Also allows Criteria1 and Criteria2 to have And or Or logical operators. Values may include xlAnd, xlBottom10Items, xlBottom10Percent, xlOr, xlTop10Items, or xlTop10Percent.

Returns
N/A

Immediate Window Sample
```
Selection.AutoFilter Field:=1, Criteria1:="1/1/97"
Selection.AutoFilter ' Toggles autofilter off
```

SEE ALSO   ActiveSheet, ActiveWorkbook

Calculate Method

Executes the calculation if the application options are set to manually recalculate

Description
The Calculate method is useful for applications that have many complex expressions. Using the Calculate method allows you to add a button to the sheet or to calculate programmatically only in particular situations. For speed of execution, it is often useful in an

automated solution to turn off automatic calculation when a number of values are being inserted into a sheet by a program.

AVAILABLE IN VB SCRIPT

Syntax
[Application.] Calculate

Parameters
N/A

Returns
N/A

Immediate Window Sample
Application.Calculate

SEE ALSO   Calculation

Calculation Property

Holds the mode of calculation for open spreadsheets

Description
This property determines when changes to a sheet will recalculate. Three modes are available: xlCalculationAutomatic, xlCalculationManual, or xlCalculationSemiautomatic. Setting the mode to manual can speed value insertion.

AVAILABLE IN VB SCRIPT

Syntax
[Application.] Calculation

Parameters
N/A

Returns
N/A

Immediate Window Sample

```
Application.Calculation = xlCalculationManual
```

SEE ALSO   Calculate

Cells Method

3

Allows row and column number access to information stored in a particular cell

Description

This method provides a quick way to access information stored in a cell by its ordinal index values. When creating a program to access individual cells, using this method is often much faster than selecting a range of cells and then retrieving or setting values. The Immediate window example will print the value stored in the cell in row 10, column 8.

AVAILABLE IN VB SCRIPT

Syntax

```
sheetname.Cells(row,col)
```

Parameters

row   Long value containing the row number to access

col   Long value containing the column number to access

Returns

Object type

Immediate Window Sample

```
? ActiveSheet.Cells(10,8).Value
```

SEE ALSO   Value

Close Method

Closes a window or a workbook

Description

The Close method is used to close a window (which requires no parameters) or to close a workbook (which can specify saving and routing information).

AVAILABLE IN VB SCRIPT

Syntax

`[object.] Close([savechanges,filename,routeworkbook])`

Parameters

savechanges   Boolean. Specifies whether changes should be saved to current filename or the one specified in the filename parameter. If parameter is omitted, user is prompted to save changes.

filename   Filename to save changes into.

routeworkbook   Boolean. Specifies whether changes should be routed. If parameter is omitted, user is prompted for routing instructions.

Returns

N/A

Immediate Window Sample

```
ActiveWorkbook.Close(True,"C:\Changes.xls")
ActiveWindow.Close
```

SEE ALSO   ActiveSheet, ActiveWorkbook

ColorIndex Property

Holds the color of a border, font, or interior for a cell or group of cells

Description

The ColorIndex specifies a color based on its position within the Excel palette. For a font, the constant xlColorIndexAutomatic can be used to have the font filled in the default color. An interior can use either the constant xlColorIndexAutomatic or xlColorIndexNone to specify the types of fill.

For the numbers of the other color indexes, see the Excel VBA help file under the ColorIndex entry. Several primary colors in the default Excel color palette include black = 1, white = 2, red = 3, light green = 4, blue = 5, yellow = 6, purple = 7, light blue = 8, dark red = 9, and green = 10.

3

AVAILABLE IN VB SCRIPT

Syntax

```
[object.] ColorIndex = indexnum
```

Parameters

indexnum   Palette index value

Returns

N/A

Immediate Window Sample

```
Selection.Interior.ColorIndex = 6
```

SEE ALSO   Value, ActiveCell, Cells, Selection

Copy Method

Copies the contents of the current object to the Clipboard or to a different part of the worksheet or workbook

Description

This method can be used to copy a selection or object to the Clipboard, to a range within a workbook, or to a worksheet within a workbook.

AVAILABLE IN VB SCRIPT

Syntax
```
object.Copy
object.Copy(destination)
object.Copy(before,after)
```

Parameters
destination   Range object to which selection will be copied.

before   Worksheet that the sheet will be copied before. If before is specified, after should remain blank.

after   Worksheet that the sheet will be copied after. If after is specified, the before parameter should remain blank.

Returns
N/A

Immediate Window Sample
```
Selection.Copy
Selection.Copy(Cells(5,5))
```

SEE ALSO   ActiveSheet, ActiveWorkbook, AutoFilter

CutCopyMode Property

Determines the Cut or Copy mode in relation to the shimmering selection box

Description
This property can be used to set or abort a cut or copy of the current selection. When in Cut or Copy mode, the border on the specified range shimmers. The property reacts differently when it is accessed and when it is set. When read from, the value can be equal to False (not in either mode), xlCopy (in Copy mode), or xlCut (in Cut mode).

When setting the property, a False cancels the current mode. On the Windows platform, setting a True value also cancels the mode, but on the Macintosh this also copies the current contents to the Clipboard.

AVAILABLE IN VB SCRIPT

Syntax

```
[Application.] CutCopyMode = mode
```

Parameters

mode   Can be equal to a Boolean value (True or False) or xlCopy or xlCut constants

Returns

N/A

Immediate Window Sample

```
Application.CutCopyMode=False
```

SEE ALSO   Copy

Delete Method

Deletes an object or range

Description

Delete can be used to eliminate a specified object or information in a range of cells. When specifying a range to delete, the type of shift (up or left) to the surrounding cells may be passed.

AVAILABLE IN VB SCRIPT

Syntax

```
[object.] Delete
[object.] Delete(shift)
```

Parameters

shift   Direction to shift remaining cells after range is deleted. May be the constants xlShiftToLeft or xlShiftUp.

Returns

N/A

Immediate Window Sample

```
Cells(1,1).Delete
Cells(1,1).EntireRow.Delete
```

SEE ALSO   Cells, Select

DisplayAlerts Property

Property that determines if dialog alerts will be displayed during code execution

Description

The property can be set to False to eliminate a lengthy process from halting for user response. If set to False, the assigned default action for each dialog will be taken. This property does not automatically reset when your program's execution has completed, so be sure to reset it to the appropriate value.

AVAILABLE IN VB SCRIPT

Syntax

```
[Application.]DisplayAlerts = True|False
```

Parameters

N/A

Returns

N/A

Immediate Window Sample

```
DisplayAlerts=False
```

SEE ALSO   ScreenUpdating, Close

End Method

Returns a range of the destination when the specified direction is taken

Description

Using the End method is equivalent to pressing the END key and an arrow key. For example, calling the End method with a range starting at A1 in the down direction will return the last cell available in that column.

AVAILABLE IN VB SCRIPT

Syntax

```
range.End(direction)
```

Parameters

direction   Direction to find the end. Can be one of the following constants: xlToLeft, xlToRight, xlUp, or xlDown.

Returns

N/A

Immediate Window Sample

```
Range("C8").End(xlUp).Select
Range("C1").End(xlDown).Select
```

SEE ALSO   Range, Select

FontStyle Property

Holds the style attributes of the Font object

Description

The style of a font can be set by using this property. Note that the Bold and Italic properties of the Font object affect and are affected by this property. Setting the Bold property to True will make the "Bold" string appear in the FontStyle string.

AVAILABLE IN VB SCRIPT

Syntax
```
font.FontStyle = styleString
```

Parameters
styleString   String of styles used separated by a space

Returns
N/A

Immediate Window Sample
```
? Selection.Font.FontStyle
Selection.Font.FontStyle = "Bold"
Selection.Font.FontStyle = "Bold Italic"
```

SEE ALSO   Selection

Formula Property

This property allows you to set specifications or to retrieve the formula for a range

Description
Any standard formula can be entered into the Formula property. Setting the Formula property to a particular string is equivalent to typing the equal (=) sign before a formula in a cell.

AVAILABLE IN VB SCRIPT

Syntax
```
cell.Formula = formula
```

Parameters
formula   Valid standard format formula string

Returns
N/A

Immediate Window Sample
```
ActiveCell.Formula = "=A1+10"
```

SEE ALSO   ActiveCell, FormulaR1C1

FormulaR1C1 Property

3

Allows you to set specifications or to retrieve the formula for a range in Row and Col format

Description
Row and column format allows formulas to be easily created that access cells relative to them. For example, the Immediate window sample demonstrates a formula that retrieves the value from one column previous to it and adds the number 10.

AVAILABLE IN VB SCRIPT

Syntax
```
range.FormulaR1C1 = formula
```

Parameters
formula   Valid formula string in row and column format

Returns
N/A

Immediate Window Sample
```
ActiveCell.FormulaR1C1 = "=RC[-1]+10"
```

SEE ALSO   Formula, ActiveCell

HorizontalAlignment Property

Determines the horizontal alignment of an object (most often a range or style)

Description

This property can be used to set the justification of a range, style, chart title, label, and so on. The following constants determine the type of alignment: xlHAlignCenter, xlHAlignDistributed, xlHAlignJustify, xlHAlignLeft, or xlHAlignRight. For range and style objects, the following constants may also be used: xlHAlignCenterAcrossSelection, xlHAlignFill, or xlHAlignGeneral.

AVAILABLE IN VB SCRIPT

Syntax

```
object.HorizontalAlignment = alignVal
```

Parameters

alignVal   Alignment constant, including xlHAlignCenter, xlHAlignDistributed, xlHAlignJustify, xlHAlignLeft, xlHAlignRight, xlHAlignCenterAcrossSelection, xlHAlignFill, or xlHAlignGeneral

Returns

Long type

Immediate Window Sample

```
Selection.HorizontalAlignment = xlHAlignLeft
Selection.HorizontalAlignment = xlHAlignRight
```

SEE ALSO   Selection, VerticalAlignment

Insert Method

Used to insert cells into a worksheet or characters before a string

Description

Using this method with a worksheet will shift the cells in the specified direction. On a string, the characters will be inserted preceding the current string.

AVAILABLE IN VB SCRIPT

Syntax

```
[object.] Insert(shift)
[object.] Insert(insertString)
```

Parameters

shift   Direction to shift the existing cells. Use the constants xlShiftToRight or xlShiftDown to specify the direction.

insertString   String of characters to insert preceding current string.

Returns

N/A

Immediate Window Sample

```
Selection.Insert(xlShiftDown)
ActiveCell.EntireRow.Insert
```

SEE ALSO   ActiveSheet, Selection, Delete

LineStyle Property

Sets the line style for a Border object

Description

Excel allows seven different line styles to be specified for individual parts of a border for a cell. Using this property, a subroutine could easily be created to automate the creation of a line form for reuse in Excel documents.

AVAILABLE IN VB SCRIPT

Syntax

```
border.LineStyle = borderType
```

Parameters

borderType   The type of border for the selected border sides. Use the following constants to specify the border style: xlContinuous, xlDash, xlDashDot, xlDashDotDot, xlDot, xlDouble, xlSlantDashDot, or xlLineStyleNone.

Returns

Variant type

Immediate Window Sample

```
Selection.Borders(xlEdgeBottom).LineStyle = xlDouble
```

SEE ALSO   ActiveSheet, Selection

Move Method

Moves a sheet within a workbook

Description

To move a sheet using this method, you must specify the sheet either before or after which the selected sheet is to be placed. If the before parameter is specified, the after parameter should be left empty and vice versa.

AVAILABLE IN VB SCRIPT

Syntax

```
sheet.Move(before,after)
```

Parameters

before   Object reference to a sheet that the specified sheet will be placed before

after   Object reference to a sheet that the specified sheet will be placed after

Returns

N/A

Immediate Window Sample

```
ActiveSheet.Move ,Sheets("Sheet3")
```

SEE ALSO   ActiveSheet, Close

Name Property

Holds the name of the object that can be used to programmatically reference it

Description

The Name property holds the string of the name used to reference an object. Instead of using an index with a collection, the name can be used to specify the object.

AVAILABLE IN VB SCRIPT

Syntax

```
object.Name = string
```

Parameters

string   Any string conforming to the standard naming conventions

Returns

N/A

Immediate Window Sample

```
? ActiveWorkbook.Name
Sheets("Sheet1").Name = "MySheet"
ActiveSheet.Name = "MySheet"
```

SEE ALSO   Value, ActiveSheet

NumberFormat Property

Determines the display format for labels, cells, and styles

Description

This property will specify the appearance of the value in the label or cell. Formatting characters (# / , 0) and value characters (m, d, y, hh, mm, ss) are the same as those used in the format cell dialog box.

AVAILABLE IN VB SCRIPT

Syntax
```
object.NumberFormat = stringVal
```

Parameters
stringVal   Formatting string containing codes of format to display value

Returns
N/A

Immediate Window Sample
```
ActiveCell.Value = 12
ActiveCell.NumberFormat = "General"
ActiveCell.NumberFormat = "hh:mm:ss m/d/yy"
ActiveCell.NumberFormat = _
"$###,##0.00_);[Blue]($###,##0.00)"
```

SEE ALSO   Range, ActiveCell

Pattern Property

Determines the pattern for either a FillFormat object or an Interior object

Description
Setting this property will change the display fill of the specified object. If the object is an Interior object (such as the one used by cells), you must use one of the following constants: xlPatternAutomatic, xlPatternChecker, xlPatternCrissCross, xlPatternDown, xlPatternGray16, xlPatternGray25, xlPatternGray50, xlPatternGray75, xlPatternGray8, xlPatternGrid, xlPatternHorizontal, xlPatternLightDown, xlPatternLightHorizontal, xlPatternLightUp, xlPatternLightVertical, xlPatternNone, xlPatternSemiGray75, xlPatternSolid, xlPatternUp, or xlPatternVertical.

For a FillFormat object, the property may be set to msoPattern5Percent, msoPattern10Percent, msoPattern20Percent, msoPattern25Percent, msoPattern30Percent, msoPattern40Percent, msoPattern50Percent, msoPattern60Percent, msoPattern70Percent, msoPattern75Percent, msoPattern80Percent, msoPattern90Percent, msoPatternDarkDownwardDiagonal, msoPatternDarkHorizontal, msoPatternDarkUpwardDiagonal, msoPatternDarkVertical, msoPatternDashedDownwardDiagonal, msoPatternDashedHorizontal, msoPatternDashedUpwardDiagonal, msoPatternDashedVertical, msoPatternDiagonalBrick, msoPatternDivot, msoPatternDottedGrid, msoPatternHorizontalBrick, msoPatternLargeCheckerBoard, msoPatternLargeConfetti, msoPatternLargeGrid, msoPatternLightDiamonds, msoPatternLightDownwardDiagonal, msoPatternLightHorizontal, msoPatternLightUpwardDiagonal, msoPatternLightVertical, msoPatternMixed, msoPatternNarrowHorizontal, msoPatternNarrowVertical, msoPatternOutlinedDiamonds, msoPatternPlaid, msoPatternShingles, msoPatternSmallCheckerBoard, msoPatternSmallConfetti, msoPatternSmallGrid, msoPatternSolidDiamonds, msoPatternSpheres, msoPatternTrellis, msoPatternWaves, msoPatternWavyLines, msoPatternWeave, msoPatternWideDownwardDiagonal, or msoPatternWideUpwardDiagonal.

AVAILABLE IN VB SCRIPT

Syntax
```
object.Pattern = patternVal
```

Parameters
patternVal   One of the available constants for the FillFormat or Interior object

Returns
Long type

Immediate Window Sample
```
ActiveCell.Interior.Pattern = xlPatternGray25
```

SEE ALSO   ActiveSheet, Range, ColorIndex

Range Object

Used to access one or more cells—most common object used in Excel

Description

Most programming in Excel uses the Range object to access cell values, appearance, and operation. Ranges may be specified by using cell notation or the Cells method, or by denoting them as named values.

AVAILABLE IN VB SCRIPT

Syntax

N/A

Parameters

N/A

Returns

N/A

Immediate Window Sample

```
Range("A1").Value = 10
Range("A2") = 10
Range("A3") = "Hello"
Range("A1:A8").Formula = "=Rand()"
```

SEE ALSO DisplayAlerts, ActiveCell, Cells

ScreenUpdating Property

Toggles whether updates are displayed on the screen

Description

Displaying updates takes a great deal of processor time. If the updates are switched off for the duration of a macro execution, the execution time may be greatly diminished. Make sure that you turn updates back on when processing is complete, because Excel does not automatically return to Normal mode.

AVAILABLE IN VB SCRIPT

Syntax

```
Application.ScreenUpdating = True|False
```

Parameters
N/A

Returns
N/A

Immediate Window Sample
```
Application.ScreenUpdating = False
```

SEE ALSO   DisplayAlerts

Select Method

Selects an object such as a cell, workbook, chart, or worksheet

Description
Use the Select method to select an object, particularly a range of cells. Use the Activate method instead for a single cell. The Select method can also be used with a replace parameter to indicate the current selection will be replaced by the specified object.

AVAILABLE IN VB SCRIPT

Syntax
```
object.Select([replace])
```

Parameters
replace   Optional. Boolean. If True, current selection is replaced by specified object.

Returns
N/A

Immediate Window Sample
```
Sheets("Sheet3").Select
Range("A1:A8").Select
```

SEE ALSO   Activate, ActiveSheet, ActiveWorkbook

Value Property

Holds a value for a particular object

Description

The Value property is used extensively within the Excel object model, particularly for setting and retrieving the values of cells.

AVAILABLE IN VB SCRIPT

Syntax

```
object.Value = value
```

Parameters

value   Dependent on the object

Returns

N/A

Immediate Window Sample

```
? ActiveCell.Value
```

SEE ALSO   Range, Select, Name

VerticalAlignment Property

Determines the horizontal alignment of an object (most often a range or style)

Description

This property can be used to set the justification of a range, style, chart title, label, and so on. The following constants determine the type of alignment: xlVAlignBottom, xlVAlignCenter, xlVAlignDistributed, xlVAlignJustify, or xlVAlignTop.

AVAILABLE IN VB SCRIPT

Syntax

```
object.VerticalAlignment = alignVal
```

Parameters

alignVal   Alignment constant, including xlVAlignBottom, xlVAlignCenter, xlVAlignDistributed, xlVAlignJustify, or xlVAlignTop

Returns

Long type

Immediate Window Sample

```
Selection.VerticalAlignment = xlVAlignBottom
Selection.VerticalAlignment = xlVAlignCenter
```

SEE ALSO   Selection, HorizontalAlignment

Weight Property

Determines the weight or thickness of the border of a range

Description

Setting the Weight property for a Border or LineFormat object will determine how the cell or range of cells appears.

AVAILABLE IN VB SCRIPT

Syntax

```
border.Weight = lineWeight
```

Parameters

lineWeight   Weight of the border should be one of these constants: xlHairline, xlThin, xlMedium, or xlThick

Returns

Long type

Immediate Window Sample

```
Selection.Borders.Weight = xlMedium
```

SEE ALSO   Pattern, Range, Selection

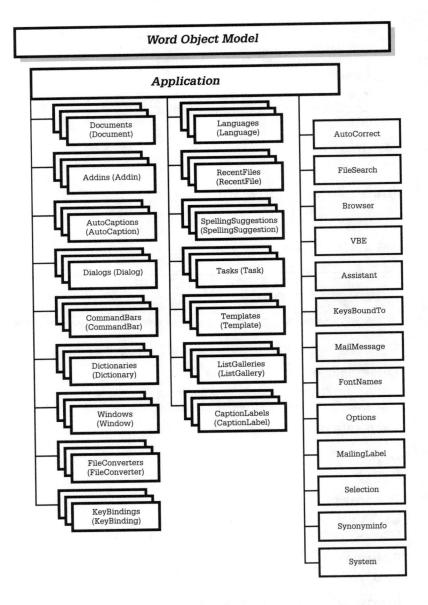

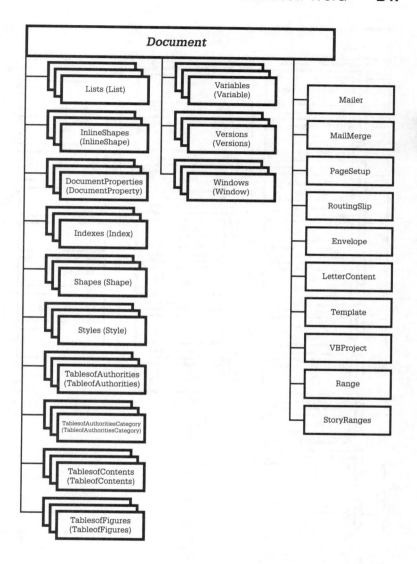

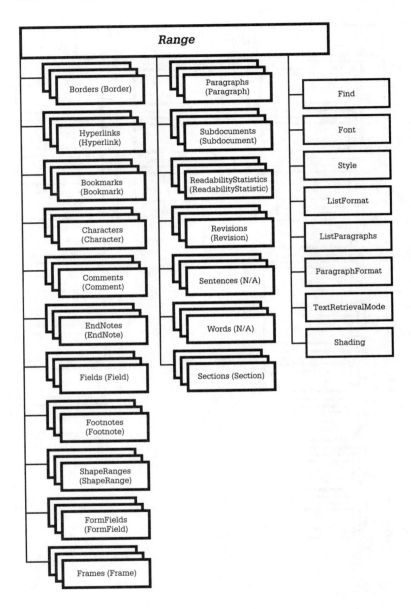

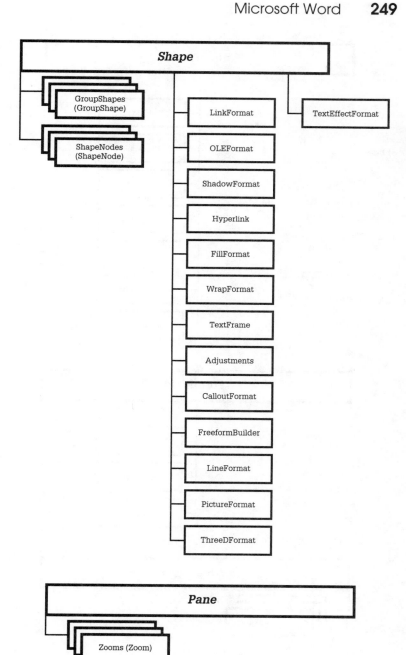

3

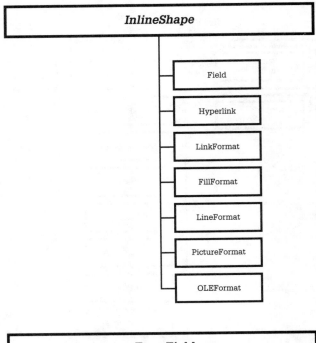

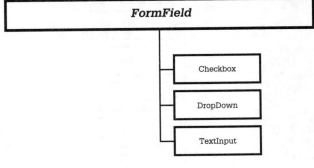

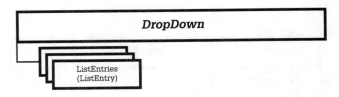

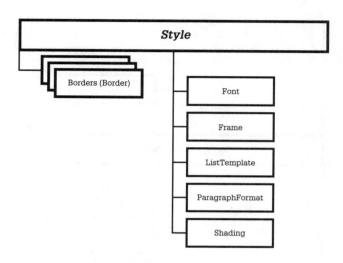

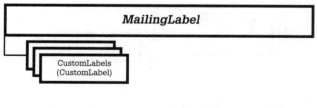

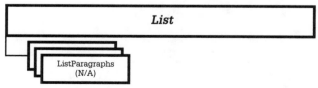

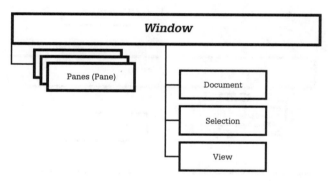

3

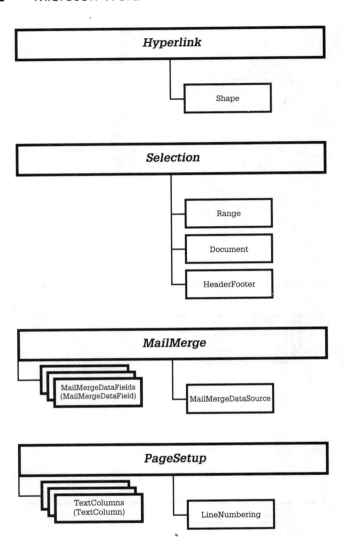

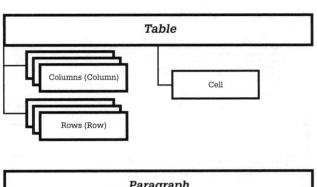

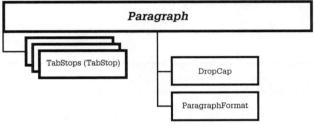

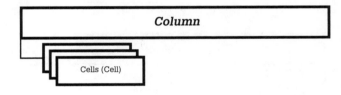

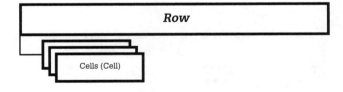

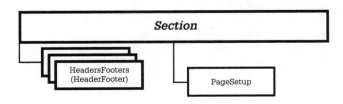

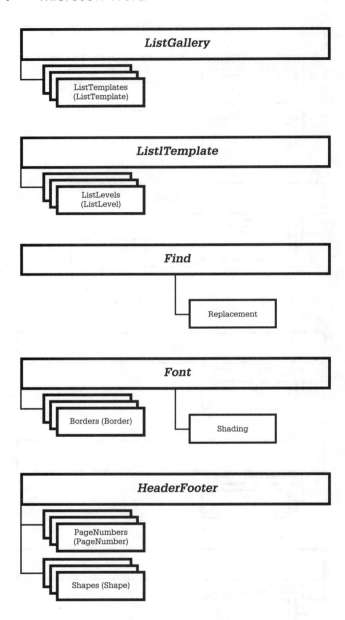

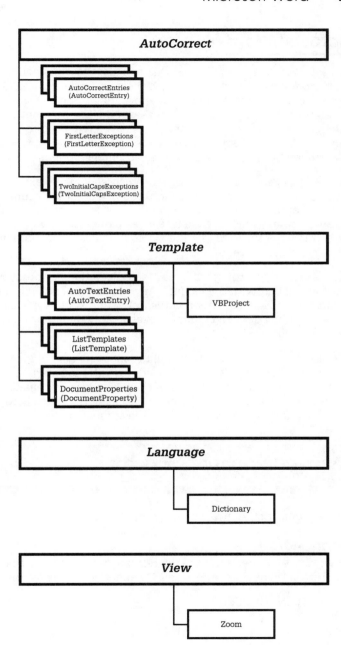

Microsoft Word

Microsoft Word is the application that has most recently added object capabilities. Therefore, the Word object model is often not as intuitive to understand as the other applications. Some of the methods of achieving solutions may seem odd. Try frequently recording test macros of the types of tasks you will need to automate. By examining the code the recorder generates, you can better understand how Word needs to accomplish things.

Also, if objects such as paragraphs are accessed, macro execution slows dramatically when advancing through a lengthy document. What may appear to execute well on the first ten paragraphs may take substantially longer when it reaches paragraph 200. Therefore, make sure you test the macro in real-world conditions in case optimization is required.

Note that when recording with the Macro Recorder in Word, you cannot select text with the mouse. Only keyboard selections are available. Using a combination of the arrow and shift keys should allow almost any desired operation. Presumably the next version of Word will resolve this problem.

Word files are stored in the Documents collection as individual objects. The text itself can be accessed through the Paragraphs collection, but it is most often easier to make necessary changes to the document with selection functions. Some of the Immediate window examples demonstrate this type of functionality.

ActiveDocument Property

Holds the object reference to the current active document

Description

This property can be used to easily reference the currently selected document in Word. A reference to a Document object is returned.

AVAILABLE IN VB SCRIPT

Syntax

```
[Application.] ActiveDocument
```

Parameters
N/A

Returns
Document object

Immediate Window Sample
```
? ActiveDocument.Name
Documents(1).Activate
? ActiveDocument.Name
```

SEE ALSO   Add

Add Method

3

Used to add an object to a particular collection

Description
The Add method can be used, as shown in the Immediate window
example, to add a new document to the current Word environment.

AVAILABLE IN VB SCRIPT

Syntax
```
object.Add
```

Parameters
N/A

Returns
N/A

Immediate Window Sample
```
Documents.Add
```

User Tip
The parameters accepted by the Add method vary depending on
the object used. For example, when adding a new document, you
can specify a template that the new document should be created

from. Check the Object Browser for the actual parameters that may be used.

SEE ALSO   Open, RecentFile

Alignment Property

Holds the alignment of a paragraph

Description

The type of alignment specified within the Alignment property is held in a number of constants within the Word system. In the Immediate window example, the currently selected paragraph is set to a center alignment.

AVAILABLE IN VB SCRIPT

Syntax

```
object.Alignment = align
```

Parameters

align   A valid alignments constant, such as wdAlignParagraphCenter, wdAlignParagraphLeft, wdAlignParagraphRight, and so on

Returns

N/A

Immediate Window Sample

```
Selection.ParagraphFormat.Alignment = _
wdAlignParagraphCenter
```

SEE ALSO   Selection

ApplyBulletDefault Method

Toggles the list formatting for a specified paragraph or range

Description

This method, when executed on a paragraph that is specified as a list, turns list formatting off. To a normal paragraph, list formatting is applied. This method must be used on a ListFormat object of a Range object.

AVAILABLE IN VB SCRIPT

Syntax

```
listformat.ApplyBulletDefault
```

Parameters

N/A

Returns

N/A

Immediate Window Sample

```
Selection.Range.ListFormat.ApplyBulletDefault
ActiveDocument.Paragraphs(2).Range.ListFormat. _
ApplyBulletDefault
```

SEE ALSO   ActiveDocument, Range

Assistant Property

Accesses the animated Assistant to allow custom help for an application

Description

The animated Assistant seems to inspire both love and hate from Office users, but programmers will find controlling the Assistant fairly easy. Animation may be set using constants such as msoAnimationSearching, msoAnimationAppear, msoAnimationGestureDown, msoAnimationIdle, msoAnimationGreeting, or msoAnimationBeginSpeaking.

AVAILABLE IN VB SCRIPT

Syntax
```
[Application.] Assistant
```

Parameters
N/A

Returns
N/A

Immediate Window Sample
```
Assistant.Visible = True
Assistant.Animation = msoAnimationSearching
Assistant.Move 100, 100
```

SEE ALSO   N/A

CheckSpelling Method

Activates the spelling checker for the current document

Description
A program can activate the spell checking on a document as well as specifying one or more custom dictionaries to check against.

AVAILABLE IN VB SCRIPT

Syntax
```
document.CheckSpelling([CustomDictionary])
```

Parameters
CustomDictionary   Specify a valid custom dictionary

Returns
N/A

Immediate Window Sample
```
ActiveDocument.CheckSpelling
```

SEE ALSO   DisplayAlerts

Compare Method

Sets up a comparison and shows comparison marks on specified document

Description

The Microsoft Word feature that allows comparison of two documents can be activated by use of this method. The filename of the document to be compared and comparison marks are automatically displayed.

AVAILABLE IN VB SCRIPT

Syntax

```
[Application.] Compare fileName
```

Parameters

fileName   Name of the file to compare to specified document

Returns

N/A

Immediate Window Sample

```
ActiveDocument.Compare "C:\draft1.doc"
```

SEE ALSO   ActiveDocument

ComputeStatistics Method

Recalculates statistics for specified range or document

Description

This method will calculate the statistics either for the entire document or a specified range. Parameters allow the inclusion/exclusion of footnotes and endnotes and the specification of exactly the type of statistic to return.

AVAILABLE IN VB SCRIPT

Syntax

```
statValue = [object.] ComputeStatistics(statistic [,
includefootnotesandendnotes])
```

Parameters

statistic   Determines the type of statistic to be returned. Use one of these constants: wdStatisticCharacters, wdStatisticCharactersWithSpaces, wdStatisticLines, wdStatisticPages, wdStatisticParagraphs, or wdStatisticWords.

includefootnotesandendnotes   Determines whether footnotes and endnotes are included. Default is set to False.

statValue   Calculated return of type specified with statistic parameter.

Returns

Long type

Immediate Window Sample

```
? ActiveDocument.ComputeStatistics(wdStatisticPages)
```

SEE ALSO   ActiveDocument

FirstLineIndent Property

Determines the indent of the first line of the paragraph

Description

Specified in points, this property holds the first line indent value. This property may be set for individual paragraphs, styles, or a range of paragraphs.

AVAILABLE IN VB SCRIPT

Syntax

```
paragraph FirstLineIndent = indentVal
```

Parameters

indentVal   In points, the value to indent on the first line of the paragraph

Returns

Variant type

Immediate Window Sample

```
ActiveDocument.Paragraphs(1).FirstLineIndent = 72
ActiveDocument.Paragraphs(1).FirstLineIndent= _
InchesToPoints(1)
```

SEE ALSO   ActiveDocument, Paragraphs

FollowHyperlink Method

Displays the specified hyperlink

Description

This method uses a link to move to another document or place within a document. As with Web browsing, if the document is cached, it is used. If not, the link is resolved and the document retrieved. If Word is not the default browser, a Web browser will be launched to display the document.

AVAILABLE IN VB SCRIPT

Syntax

```
document.FollowHyperlink(Address [, SubAddress]
[, NewWindow] [, AddHistory] [, ExtraInfo] [, Method]
[, HeaderInfo])
```

Parameters

Address   Address of document to follow.

SubAddress   Location with the target document, such as an anchor.

NewWindow   Boolean to specify whether document should be opened in a new window.

AddHistory Reserved for future use.

ExtraInfo Additional information (such as ImageMap coordinates) to be sent to the server.

Method Determines how additional information is handled. Use either the msoMethodGet or the msoMethodPost constant.

HeaderInfo HTTP header information.

Returns
N/A

Immediate Window Sample
```
ActiveDocument.FollowHyperlink _
"http://www.microsoft.com"
ActiveDocument.FollowHyperlink _
"http://www.cvisual.com"
```

SEE ALSO ActiveDocument

Font Object

Holds all of the font formatting information for a piece of text

Description
The Font object can be set to any available font, size, and style settings that are normally available in Word. The Immediate window example changes the font of the current selection in a variety of ways.

AVAILABLE IN VB SCRIPT

Syntax
```
range.Font
```

Parameters
N/A

Returns
N/A

Immediate Window Sample

```
Selection.Font.Name = "Times New Roman"
Selection.Font.Size = 10
Selection.Font.Bold = True
Selection.Font.Italic = True
```

SEE ALSO   Selection

Height Property

Holds the height of the specified object

Description

The height of most objects may be adjusted with the Height property, including shapes, rows, cols, tasks, windows, frames, custom labels, inline shapes, and so on.

AVAILABLE IN VB SCRIPT

Syntax

```
object.Height = height
```

Parameters

height   Height value within the limits of the object. Value is stored as a Single type.

Returns

N/A

Immediate Window Sample

```
ActiveWindow.WindowState = wdWindowStateNormal
ActiveWindow.Height = ActiveWindow.Height / 2
```

User Tip

Using the Width and Height properties to configure the windows allows you to create a custom macro to adjust the window settings to the sizes you most commonly use.

SEE ALSO   Width

InsertBefore Method

Inserts text before the indicated object

Description

The InsertBefore method may be used with either a Range or Selection to insert text into the document. The Immediate example demonstrates inserting the word "Hello" before the first word of the first paragraph of the document.

AVAILABLE IN VB SCRIPT

Syntax

`object.InsertBefore(string)`

Parameters

string   Any valid Unicode string

Returns

N/A

Immediate Window Sample

```
ActiveDocument.Range.Paragraphs(1).Range.Words(1). _
InsertBefore "Hello"
```

SEE ALSO   Selection

LeftIndent Property

Determines the left indent of the specified paragraph, styles, or range of paragraphs

Description

This property will specify the left indent of a particular paragraph, range, or style. The indent is specified in points (1 inch = 72 points).

AVAILABLE IN VB SCRIPT

Syntax
```
paragraph.LeftIndent = leftValue
```

Parameters
leftValue   Amount in points to left-indent the paragraph

Returns
Single type

Immediate Window Sample
```
ActiveDocument.Paragraphs(1).LeftIndent = 72
```

SEE ALSO   FirstIndent, RightIndent

LineSpacing Property

Determines the line spacing of the specified paragraph, styles, or range of paragraphs

Description
This property will specify the line spacing of a particular paragraph, range, or style. The spacing is specified in points (1 inch = 72 points).

AVAILABLE IN VB SCRIPT

Syntax
```
paragraph.LineSpacing = lineValue
```

Parameters
lineValue   Amount in points of the line space for the paragraph

Returns
Single type

Immediate Window Sample
```
Selection.Paragraphs.LineSpacing = 16
Selection.Paragraphs.LineSpacing = LinesToPoints(2)
```

SEE ALSO   Paragraphs

ListParagraphs Property

Holds the object reference to all of the numbered paragraphs within a range or document

Description

All of the List Paragraphs contained within a document can be accessed individually through this property. A For...Each loop can be used to sequentially progress through each list paragraph.

AVAILABLE IN VB SCRIPT

Syntax

```
document.ListParagraphs
```

Parameters

N/A

Returns

N/A

Immediate Window Sample

```
Documents(1).ListParagraphs(1).Shading _
.BackgroundPatternColorIndex = wdBlue
```

SEE ALSO ActiveDocument, Paragraphs

MoveDown Method

Moves the selection cursor down one unit

Description

The Move methods may be used with either a Range or Selection, and units and type of move may be defined. Move in units of lines, paragraphs, windows, or screens.

AVAILABLE IN VB SCRIPT

Syntax

```
object.MoveDown([,units,count [,extend]])
```

Parameters

units Move down in the units specified by the constant wdLine, wdParagraph, wdWindow, or wdScreen.

count Number of units to move selection.

extend Determines whether selection is moved or extended. Use the constant wdMove or wdExtend.

Returns

N/A

Immediate Window Sample

```
Selection.MoveDown
Selection.MoveDown wdParagraph,1
Selection.MoveDown wdParagraph,1,wdExtend
```

SEE ALSO   MoveUp, MoveLeft, MoveRight

MoveLeft Method

Moves the selection cursor left one unit

Description

The Move methods may be used with either a Range or Selection, and units and type of move may be defined. Move in units of lines, paragraphs, windows, or screens.

AVAILABLE IN VB SCRIPT

Syntax

```
object.MoveLeft([,units,count [,extend]])
```

Parameters

units Move left in the units specified by the constant wdCell, wdCharacter, wdWord, or wdSentence.

count Number of units to move selection.

extend Determines whether selection is moved or extended. Use the constant wdMove or wdExtend.

Returns
N/A

Immediate Window Sample
```
Selection.MoveLeft
Selection.MoveLeft wdCharacter,1
Selection.MoveLeft wdCharacter,1,wdExtend
```

SEE ALSO MoveDown, MoveUp, MoveRight

MoveRight Method

Moves the selection cursor right one unit

Description
The Move methods may be used with either a Range or Selection, and units and type of move may be defined. Move in units of lines, paragraphs, windows, or screens.

AVAILABLE IN VB SCRIPT

Syntax
```
object.MoveRight([,unit,count [,extend]])
```

Parameters
units Move right in the units specified by the constant wdCell, wdCharacter, wdWord, or wdSentence.

count Number of units to move selection.

extend Determines whether selection is moved or extended. Use the constant wdMove or wdExtend.

Returns
N/A

Immediate Window Sample

```
Selection.MoveRight
Selection.MoveRight wdCharacter,1
Selection.MoveRight wdCharacter,1,wdExtend
```

SEE ALSO   MoveDown, MoveUp, MoveLeft

MoveUp Method

Moves the current selection up one unit

Description

The Move methods may be used with either a Range or Selection, and units and type of move may be defined. Move in units of lines, paragraphs, windows, or screens.

AVAILABLE IN VB SCRIPT

Syntax

```
object.MoveUp([,units,count [,extend]])
```

Parameters

units   Move up in the units specified by the constant wdLine, wdParagraph, wdWindow, or wdScreen.

count   Number of units to move selection.

extend   Determines whether selection is moved or extended. Use the constant wdMove or wdExtend.

Returns

N/A

Immediate Window Sample

```
Selection.MoveUp
Selection.MoveUp wdParagraph,1
Selection.MoveUp wdParagraph,1,wdExtend
```

SEE ALSO   MoveDown, MoveLeft, MoveRight

Name Property

Holds the name of the object that can be used to programmatically reference it

Description
The Name property holds the string of the name used to reference an object. Instead of using an index with a collection, the name can be used to specify the object.

AVAILABLE IN VB SCRIPT

Syntax
```
object.Name = string
```

Parameters
string   Any string conforming to the standard naming conventions

Returns
N/A

Immediate Window Sample
```
? ActiveDocument.Name
```

User Tip
The Name property of a document is read-only. To change the name, you must use the SaveAs method.

SEE ALSO   ActiveDocument

Open Method

Opens the specified object

Description
This method can be used to open files through a number of objects (such as Documents or RecentFiles).

AVAILABLE IN VB SCRIPT

Syntax
`object.Open(filename$)`

Parameters
filename$ May specify the path and filename of any file Word can open

Returns
Object type

Immediate Window Sample
`Documents.Open "c:\mydoc.doc"`

SEE ALSO   Add

Paragraphs Collection

Holds all of the paragraphs for a particular document

Description
All of the actual text, styles, and other information for each paragraph of a document are held by the individual objects stored in the Paragraphs collection. Note that accessing long documents by paragraph can be a slow process.

AVAILABLE IN VB SCRIPT

Syntax
`object.Paragraphs(index)`

Parameters
index   Paragraph number to be accessed

Returns
N/A

Immediate Window Sample

```
? ActiveDocument.Range.Paragraphs.Count
ActiveDocument.Range.Paragraphs(1).Range.Words(1) _
= "Hello"
```

SEE ALSO   Add

RecentFile Object

Holds a reference to one of the recently accessed files

Description

The RecentFiles collection holds all of the RecentFile objects that may be opened, modified, deleted, and so on. Recent files may also be added to the collection. This is useful if a particular job requires repeated access to a set of documents. A macro can be created to insert these document names into the Recent File list.

AVAILABLE IN VB SCRIPT

Syntax

```
[Application].RecentFiles
```

Parameters

N/A

Returns

N/A

Immediate Window Sample

```
RecentFiles(2).Open
```

SEE ALSO   Open, Add

RightIndent Property

Determines the right indent of the specified paragraph, styles, or range of paragraphs

Description

This property will specify the right indent of a particular paragraph, range, or style. The indent is specified in points (1 inch = 72 points).

AVAILABLE IN VB SCRIPT

Syntax
```
paragraph.RightIndent = rightValue
```

Parameters

rightValue   Amount in points to right-indent the paragraph

Returns

Single type

Immediate Window Sample
```
Selection.Paragraphs.RightIndent = 72
```

SEE ALSO   LeftIndent

Selection Object

Holds the range of the current selection

Description

The Selection object provides access to the current user selection. Manipulating the Selection object also allows a document to be quickly and easily modified.

AVAILABLE IN VB SCRIPT

Syntax

```
[Application].Selection
```

Parameters

N/A

Returns

N/A

Immediate Window Sample

```
Selection.TypeText "Replace"
```

SEE ALSO   InsertBefore

Shading Property

Holds the reference to the Shading object used by other objects, such as paragraphs

Description

Setting properties of the Shading object can render the background, foreground, and shading texture of objects.

AVAILABLE IN VB SCRIPT

Syntax

```
object.Shading
```

Parameters

N/A

Returns

N/A

Immediate Window Sample

```
Selection.Paragraphs.Shading.Texture =
wdTexture12Pt5Percent
Selection.Paragraphs.Shading. _
BackgroundPatternColorIndex = wdRed
```

SEE ALSO   Selection

SpaceAfter Property

Determines the amount of space after a specified paragraph, styles, or range of paragraphs

Description

This property will specify the amount of space after a particular paragraph, range, or style. The spacing is specified in points (1 inch = 72 points).

AVAILABLE IN VB SCRIPT

Syntax

```
paragraph.SpaceAfter = afterValue
```

Parameters

afterValue   Amount in points of space after the paragraph

Returns

Single type

Immediate Window Sample

```
Selection.Paragraphs.SpaceAfter = 12
```

SEE ALSO   LineSpacing, SpaceBefore

SpaceBefore Property

Determines the amount of space before a specified paragraph, styles, or range of paragraphs

Description

This property will specify the amount of space before a particular paragraph, range, or style. The spacing is specified in points (1 inch = 72 points).

AVAILABLE IN VB SCRIPT

Syntax
```
paragraph.SpaceBefore = beforeValue
```

Parameters
beforeValue   Amount in points of space before the paragraph

Returns
Single type

Immediate Window Sample
```
Selection.Paragraphs.SpaceBefore = 12
```

SEE ALSO   LineSpacing, SpaceAfter

TypeBackspace Method

Backspaces at the current selection

Description
The method will provide the same functionality (including across multiple selected characters) as the user pressing the BACKSPACE key.

AVAILABLE IN VB SCRIPT

Syntax
```
object.TypeBackspace
```

Parameters
N/A

Returns
N/A

Immediate Window Sample
```
Selection.TypeBackspace
```

SEE ALSO   Selection, Paragraphs

TypeText Method

Enters text at the current selection

Description
Text is entered as if from the keyboard. This means that any currently selected text will be automatically deleted.

AVAILABLE IN VB SCRIPT

Syntax
```
object.TypeText string
```

Parameters
string   Any valid character string

Returns
N/A

Immediate Window Sample
```
Selection.TypeText "Hello World"
```

SEE ALSO   Selection, TypeBackspace, Paragraphs

Width Property

Holds the width of the specified object

Description
The width of most objects may be adjusted with the Width property, including shapes, rows, cols, tasks, windows, frames, custom labels, inline shapes, and so on.

AVAILABLE IN VB SCRIPT

Syntax
```
object.Width = width
```

Parameters

width Width value within the limits of the object. Value is stored as a Single type.

Returns

N/A

Immediate Window Sample

```
ActiveWindow.WindowState = wdWindowStateNormal
ActiveWindow.Width = ActiveWindow.Width / 2
```

SEE ALSO Height

WindowState Property

Holds the current state of the specified window

Description

This property changes the state of the specified window to be maximized, minimized, or set to normal.

AVAILABLE IN VB SCRIPT

Syntax

```
window.WindowState = state
```

Parameters

state Use the constant wdWindowStateMaximize, wdWindowStateMinimize, or wdWindowStateNormal.

Returns

N/A

Immediate Window Sample

```
ActiveWindow.WindowState = wdWindowStateNormal
```

SEE ALSO Height, Width

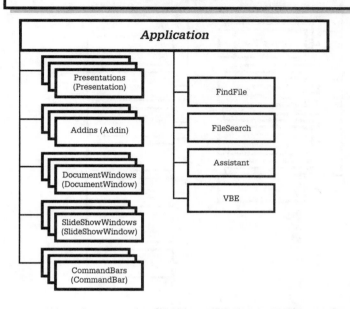

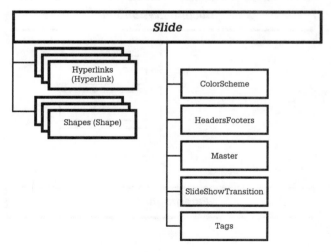

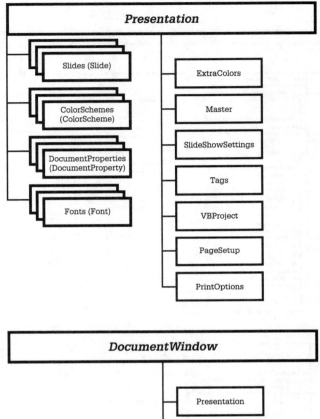

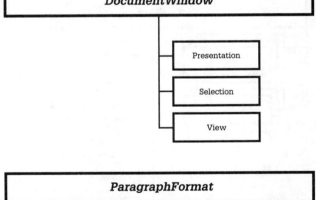

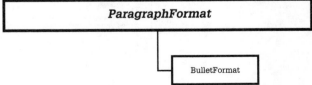

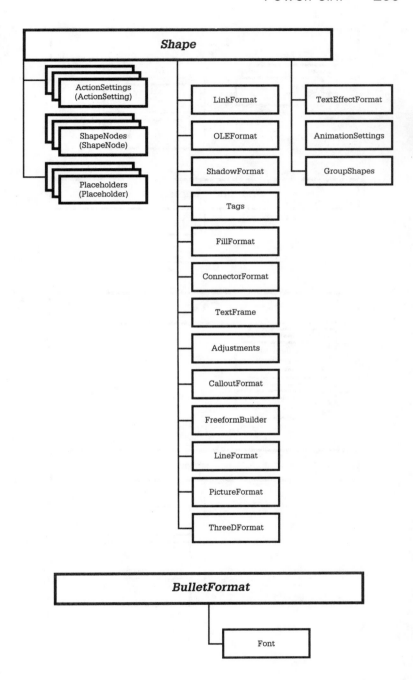

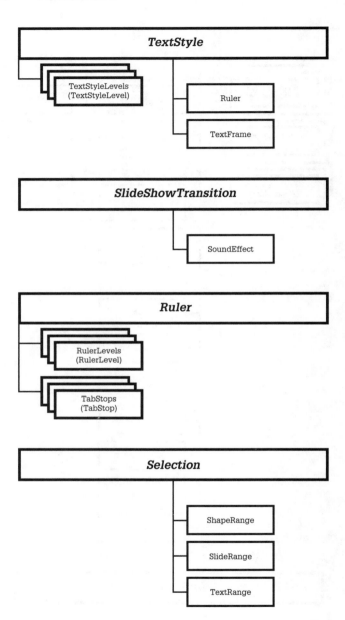

3

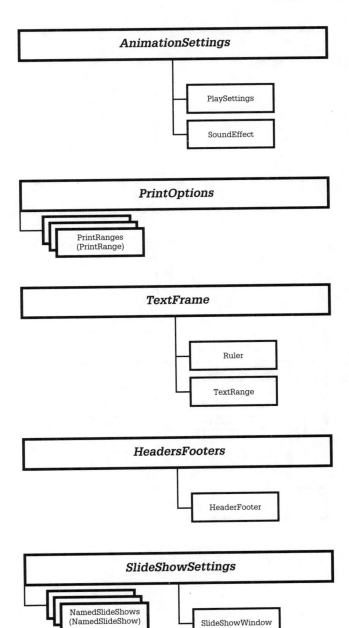

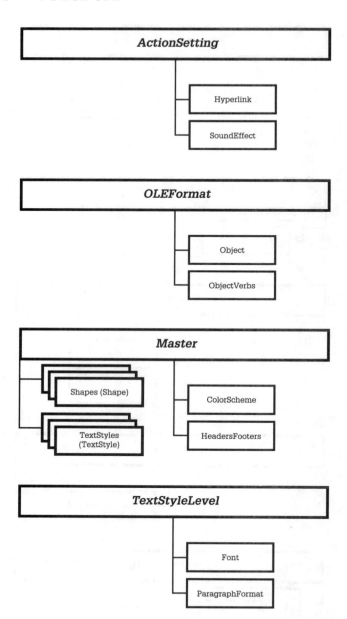

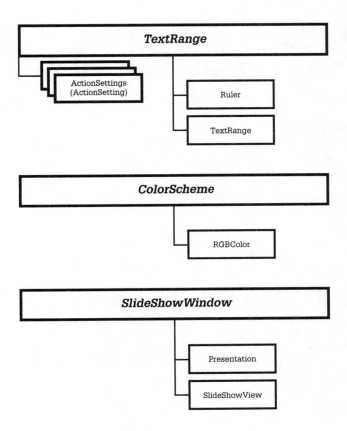

PowerPoint

The PowerPoint object model is very straightforward. The primary objects are the Presentation objects in the Presentations collection. Individual Slide objects are stored within the Slides collection. The Shape objects, while they appear standard across the Office applications, have slight variations in the context of each application. The PowerPoint implementation of the Shape object varies slightly, so examine code that is being moved from another VBA application carefully.

Many of the Immediate window examples assume that there is an open presentation that contains at least a single slide. The slide is duplicated in some commands, new objects are inserted, and so on. When running the examples, simply keep an open disposable presentation for correct execution.

Action Property

Determines the action that will be taken when an event occurs

Description
The ActionSetting object holds the complete specifications of an event, including the Action property to specify what will occur when the event happens.

AVAILABLE IN VB SCRIPT

Syntax
```
actionSetting.Action = actionType
```

Parameters
actionType   Specifies action that should take place. Use one of the following constants to specify the action: ppActionEndShow, ppActionFirstSlide, ppActionHyperlink, ppActionLastSlide, ppActionLastSlideViewed, ppActionMixed, ppActionNamedSlideShow, ppActionNextSlide, ppActionNone, ppActionOLEVerb, ppActionPreviousSlide, ppActionRunMacro, or ppActionRunProgram.

Returns
Long type

Immediate Window Sample
```
ActivePresentation.Slides(1).Shapes(1) _
.ActionSettings(ppMouseOver).Action = _
ppActionNextSlide
```

SEE ALSO   ActionVerb

ActionVerb Property

Determines the verb of the action to take place when an action event occurs

Description

The ActionVerb property works in conjunction with the Action property by specifying the verb for the action. Possible values include those shown in the Object action combo box on the Play Settings tab in the Custom Animation dialog box.

AVAILABLE IN VB SCRIPT

Syntax

```
actionSetting.ActionVerb = actionVerbType
```

Parameters

actionVerbType   String containing a verb setting such as "Play" or "Edit"

Returns

String type

Immediate Window Sample

```
ActivePresentation.Slides(1).Shapes(1) _
.ActionSettings(ppMouseOver).ActionVerb = "Play"
```

SEE ALSO   Action

AddLabel Method

Adds a Label object to the current Shapes collection

Description

This method adds a new Label shape to the Shapes collection. Other methods such as AddCallout, AddConnector, and so on, can create other shapes. The Immediate window example adds a shape and then sets the text that is displayed.

AVAILABLE IN VB SCRIPT

Syntax

```
object.AddLabel(orient,x,y,width,height)
```

Parameters

orient   Orientation available as a set of constants within PowerPoint

x, y   Single values in points for the top and left corners of the label

width, height   Single values in points for the width and height of the label

Returns

Object type

Immediate Window Sample

```
set b = ActivePresentation.Slides(1).Shapes.AddLabel( _
msoTextOrientationHorizontal,50,100,100,100) _
b.textframe.textrange.text = "Yeah"
```

SEE ALSO   Duplicate

AdvanceOnTime Property

Determines whether the slide automatically advances after AdvanceTime has been exceeded

Description

This property determines whether the slide will automatically advance to the next slide using the time stored in the AdvanceTime property.

AVAILABLE IN VB SCRIPT

Syntax

```
slide.AdvanceOnTime = onTimeFlag
```

Parameters

onTimeFlag   Boolean. Indicates whether slide should advance automatically.

Returns

Long type

Immediate Window Sample

```
ActivePresentation.Slides(1).SlideShowTransition _
.AdvanceTime = 10 ' seconds
ActivePresentation.Slides(1).SlideShowTransition _
.AdvanceOnTime = true
```

SEE ALSO   AdvanceTime

3

AdvanceTime Property

Number of seconds until automatic advance to the next slide

Description

After the AdvanceOnTime property has been set to True, this
property determines the amount of time to pause before moving to
the next slide.

AVAILABLE IN VB SCRIPT

Syntax

```
slide.AdvanceTime = onTimeValue
```

Parameters

onTimeValue   Amount in seconds to wait before continuing to the
next slide

Returns

Single type

Immediate Window Sample

```
ActivePresentation.Slides(1).SlideShowTransition _
.AdvanceTime = 10 ' seconds
ActivePresentation.Slides(1).SlideShowTransition _
.AdvanceOnTime = true
```

SEE ALSO   AdvanceOnTime

AfterEffect Property

Determines the appearance of a particular shape after it's been built

Description

Shapes can be added to a slide with animation settings. After they have been "built," this property determines their appearance. This property may be used to dim items after they are originally presented.

AVAILABLE IN VB SCRIPT

Syntax

```
animationsettings.AfterEffect = effectType
```

Parameters

effectType   The type of after effect specified by one of the following constants: ppAfterEffectDim, ppAfterEffectHide, ppAfterEffectHideOnClick, ppAfterEffectMixed, or ppAfterEffectNothing

Returns

Long type

Immediate Window Sample

```
ActivePresentation.Slides(1).Shapes.Title. _
AnimationSettings_
.AfterEffect = ppAfterEffectHide
```

SEE ALSO   Animate

Animate Property

Determines whether shape is animated

Description

Setting this property to True will enable all of the animation properties for the specified Shape object.

AVAILABLE IN VB SCRIPT

Syntax

```
animationsettings.Animate = animateFlag
```

3

Parameters

animateFlag   Boolean. True setting activates animation for this shape.

Returns

Long type

Immediate Window Sample

```
ActivePresentation.Slides(2).Shapes.Title. _
AnimationSettings _
.Animate = True
```

SEE ALSO   AfterEffect

AnimateAction Property

Determines whether color of shape is inverted when mouse event occurs

Description

The ActionSettings object determines what reaction occurs after an event. The AnimateAction property determines if the shape will be inverted when this action occurs. Using the function will make the shape invert when the action takes place, as if it was a command button. You can use this capability to add graphic buttons to your presentation.

AVAILABLE IN VB SCRIPT

Syntax

```
actionsettings.AnimateAction = actionFlag
```

Parameters

actionFlag   Boolean. Set to True if shape is inverted after action.

Returns

Long type

Immediate Window Sample

```
ActivePresentation.Slides(1).Shapes(1) _
.ActionSettings(ppMouseOver).AnimateAction = True
```

SEE ALSO   Action, ActionVerb

BeginConnect Method

Sets the beginning of the connector between two shapes

Description

PowerPoint allows a connector to be created between two shapes
that automatically adjusts when the size or position of the shapes
changes. This method sets the beginning of the connector to a
shape. The Immediate window example requires two shapes to
exist on slide 1.

AVAILABLE IN VB SCRIPT

Syntax

```
object.BeginConnect(connectedShape, connectionSite)
```

Parameters

connectedShape   Object reference to shape to begin connection

connectionSite   Site on shape to begin connection

Returns

Variant type

Immediate Window Sample

```
Set firstShape = ActivePresentation. _
Slides(1).Shapes(1)
Set secondShape = ActivePresentation. _
```

```
Slides(1).Shapes(2)
Set connect = ActivePresentation.Slides(1).Shapes _
.AddConnector(msoConnectorCurve, 0, 0, 100, 100)_
connect.connectorformat.BeginConnect firstShape, 1
connect.connectorformat.EndConnect secondShape, 1
```

SEE ALSO   Shape

BlackandWhite Property

Determines the color or black-and-white state of a specified window

Description
To see how a presentation will look when printed in black and white, this property will set a particular window to show all slides displayed in the window in this manner.

AVAILABLE IN VB SCRIPT

Syntax
```
window.BlackandWhite = bwFlag
```

Parameters
bwFlag   Boolean. Set to True to display window in black-and-white mode.

Returns
Long type

Immediate Window Sample
```
Application.Windows(1).BlackAndWhite = True
```

SEE ALSO   ColorFormat

ChartUnitEffects Property

Determines the animation effects for graphs

Description

As a graph is built with animation, this property allows the selection of animation by series, category, or element. For the animation to display, the Animate property must be set to True.

AVAILABLE IN VB SCRIPT

Syntax

```
animationsettings.ChartUnitEffects = effectType
```

Parameters

effectType This parameter determines how the chart will be animated. Use one of the following constants: ppAnimateByCategory, ppAnimateByCategoryElements, ppAnimateBySeries, ppAnimateBySeriesElements, or ppAnimateChartMixed.

Returns

Long type

Immediate Window Sample

```
ActivePresentation.Slides(1).Shapes.Title. _
AnimationSettings _
.ChartUnitEffects = True
```

SEE ALSO   Animate

Color Object

Holds the color formatting for a foreground, background, gradient, or patterned color

Description

The Color object is used with AnimationSettings, FillFormat, Font, LineFormat, ShadowFormat, SlideShowView, and ThreeDFormat objects. Colors stored in the object can be individual RGB colors or color schemes created with the SchemeColor property.

AVAILABLE IN VB SCRIPT

Syntax
`object.Color`

Parameters
N/A

Returns
N/A

Immediate Window Sample
```
ActivePresentation.Slides(1).Shapes(1).TextFrame _
.TextRange.Font.Color.SchemeColor = ppForeground
```

SEE ALSO   ActiveSheet, ActiveWorkbook

Count Property

Used to determine how many objects are in a collection

Description
The Count property can be used with a For...Next loop to cycle through all of the objects held in a collection.

AVAILABLE IN VB SCRIPT

Syntax
`object.Count`

Parameters
N/A

Returns
Long type

Immediate Window Sample
```
? ActivePresentation.Slides.Count
```

SEE ALSO   AddLabel

DeleteText Method

Deletes all of the text in a Shape object

Description
This method will eliminate all of the text stored in a TextFrame object.

AVAILABLE IN VB SCRIPT

Syntax
```
textframe.DeleteText
```

Parameters
N/A

Returns
N/A

Immediate Window Sample
```
ActivePresentation.Slides(1).Shapes(1) _
.TextFrame.DeleteText
```

SEE ALSO　AddLabel

DisplayMasterShapes Property

Determines whether slide displays shapes on slide master

Description
This property will determine if the shapes and text stored on the slide master will be displayed in the background of the current slide. The default when a new slide is created is to set this property to True. Note that setting the DisplayMasterShapes does not automatically set the slide to the master color scheme. Use the FollowMasterBackground and ColorScheme properties to ensure the slide matches.

AVAILABLE IN VB SCRIPT

Syntax
```
slide.DisplayMasterShapes = msFlag
```

Parameters
msFlag Setting this property to True will display the slide master shapes in the background.

Returns
Long type

Immediate Window Sample
```
ActivePresentation.Slides(1).DisplayMasterShapes =
True
```

SEE ALSO   RGB

DisplaySlideMiniature Property

Determines whether the slide miniature window is displayed

Description
The slide miniature window is a small window that displays what the slide will look like when presented. This window is updated in real time as changes are made to the contents of the slide in any of the viewing modes. This property determines whether the window is displayed.

AVAILABLE IN VB SCRIPT

Syntax
```
view.DisplaySlideMiniature = smFlag
```

Parameters
smFlag Boolean. Setting this property to True will display the slide miniature window.

Returns
Long type

Immediate Window Sample
```
Windows(1).View.DisplaySlideMiniature = True
```

SEE ALSO Zoom

Duplicate Method

Duplicates specified object

Description
The Duplicate method can be used within PowerPoint to make a duplicate of an object and all of the objects stored within the object. The Immediate window example demonstrates duplicating the first slide and any objects contained in it.

AVAILABLE IN VB SCRIPT

Syntax
```
object.Duplicate
```

Parameters
N/A

Returns
N/A

Immediate Window Sample
```
ActivePresentation.Slides(1).Duplicate
```

SEE ALSO AddLabel

EntryEffect Property

Determines the animation effect upon entry to the current slide

Description

This property specifies the animation effect that will be used when this slide is entered. The transition effect may be set to any of the numerous constants supplied with PowerPoint.

AVAILABLE IN VB SCRIPT

Syntax

EntryEffect = effectType

Parameters

effectType   The effects available for entry are numerous. Use any of the following constants: ppEffectAppear, ppEffectBlindsHorizontal, ppEffectBlindsVertical, ppEffectBoxIn, ppEffectBoxOut, ppEffectCheckerboardAcross, ppEffectCheckerboardDown, ppEffectCoverDown, ppEffectCoverLeft, ppEffectCoverLeftDown, ppEffectCoverLeftUp, ppEffectCoverRight, ppEffectCoverRightDown, ppEffectCoverRightUp, ppEffectCoverUp, ppEffectCrawlFromDown, ppEffectCrawlFromLeft, ppEffectCrawlFromRight, ppEffectCrawlFromUp, ppEffectCut, ppEffectCutThroughBlack, ppEffectDissolve, ppEffectFade, ppEffectFlashOnceFast, ppEffectFlashOnceMedium, ppEffectFlashOnceSlow, ppEffectFlyFromBottom, ppEffectFlyFromBottomLeft, ppEffectFlyFromBottomRight, ppEffectFlyFromLeft, ppEffectFlyFromRight, ppEffectFlyFromTop, ppEffectFlyFromTopLeft, ppEffectFlyFromTopRight, ppEffectMixed, ppEffectNone, ppEffectPeekFromDown, ppEffectPeekFromLeft, ppEffectPeekFromRight, ppEffectPeekFromUp, ppEffectRandom, ppEffectRandomBarsHorizontal, ppEffectRandomBarsVertical, ppEffectSplitHorizontalIn, ppEffectSplitHorizontalOut, ppEffectSplitVerticalIn, ppEffectSplitVerticalOut, ppEffectStripsDownLeft, ppEffectStripsDownRight, ppEffectStripsLeftDown, ppEffectStripsLeftUp, ppEffectStripsRightDown, ppEffectStripsRightUp, ppEffectStripsUpLeft, ppEffectStripsUpRight, ppEffectUncoverDown, ppEffectUncoverLeft, ppEffectUncoverLeftDown, ppEffectUncoverLeftUp, ppEffectUncoverRight, ppEffectUncoverRightDown, ppEffectUncoverRightUp, ppEffectUncoverUp, ppEffectWipeDown, ppEffectWipeLeft, ppEffectWipeRight, ppEffectWipeUp

Returns
Variant type

Immediate Window Sample
```
ActivePresentation.Slides(2).Shapes.Title. _
AnimationSettings _
.EntryEffect = ppEffectWipeLeft
```

SEE ALSO   Animate

GotoSlide Method

Changes the View to the specified slide number

Description
This method will change the slide currently displayed to the one specified. The specified slide also becomes the current active slide.

AVAILABLE IN VB SCRIPT

Syntax
```
view.GotoSlide(index)
```

Parameters
index   Long type. Number of current slide to display.

Returns
N/A

Immediate Window Sample
```
Windows(1).View.GotoSlide 2
```

SEE ALSO   EntryEffect

GradientColorType Property

Determines the gradient type of a Fill object

Description

The GradientColorType property can be used to determine the gradient type of a Fill object. Use individual methods such as PresetGradient or TwoColorGradient to set this parameter.

AVAILABLE IN VB SCRIPT

Syntax
```
fill.GradientColorType = gradType
```

Parameters

gradType   Long type. Values can be compared with the following constants: msoGradientColorMixed, msoGradientOneColor, msoGradientPresetColors, or msoGradientTwoColors.

Returns

Long type

Immediate Window Sample
```
? ActivePresentation.Slides(1).Shapes(1) _
.Fill.GradientColorType
```

SEE ALSO   PresetGradient, TwoColorGradient

GradientDegree Property

Determines the darkness or lightness of a one-color gradient in a Fill object

Description

This property varies in value from 0 (black mixed with foreground color) to 1 (white mixed with foreground color). Decimals determine the degree of mixing.

AVAILABLE IN VB SCRIPT

Syntax
```
fill.GradientDegree
```

Parameters
N/A

Returns
Single type

Immediate Window Sample
```
? ActivePresentation.Slides(1).Shapes(1) _
.Fill.GradientDegree
```

SEE ALSO   PresetGradient

GradientStyle Property

Determines the style/direction of the gradient fill of a Fill object

Description
The GradientStyle property is read-only and can be set by use of one of the gradient fill methods. The style affects the direction and appearance of the gradient. An error will be generated by the Fill object if this property is accessed when the fill does not contain a gradient.

AVAILABLE IN VB SCRIPT

Syntax
```
fill.GradientStyle = gradStyle
```

Parameters
gradStyle   This property may be compared against one of the following constants: msoGradientDiagonalDown, msoGradientDiagonalUp, msoGradientFromCenter, msoGradientFromCorner, msoGradientFromTitle, msoGradientHorizontal, msoGradientMixed, or msoGradientVertical.

Returns
Long type

Immediate Window Sample

```
? ActivePresentation.Slides(1).Shapes(1) _
.Fill.GradientStyle
```

SEE ALSO   PresetGradient, TwoColorGradient

HideWhileNotPlaying Property

3

Determines whether a multimedia clip is hidden when not playing

Description

The HideWhileNotPlaying property determines whether the media clip is hidden when not playing. The Immediate window example requires the first object on the first slide to be a media clip.

AVAILABLE IN VB SCRIPT

Syntax

```
playsettings.HideWhileNotPlaying = hpFlag
```

Parameters

hpFlag   Boolean. Set to True if media clip should be hidden while not playing.

Returns

Long type

Immediate Window Sample

```
ActivePresentation.Slides(1).Shapes(1). _
AnimationSettings _
.PlaySettings.HideWhileNotPlaying = True
```

SEE ALSO   Animate, LoopUntilStopped

Hyperlink Property

Provides reference to the Hyperlink object for hyperlink connections

Description

A Hyperlink can be used to jump to an HTTP site, to a file, or to another presentation. By use of this property, a shape can be configured to act as a hyperlink when a specific event occurs.

AVAILABLE IN VB SCRIPT

Syntax

```
object.Hyperlink
```

Parameters

N/A

Returns

Hyperlink object type

Immediate Window Sample

```
ActivePresentation.Slides(1).Shapes(1) _
.ActionSettings(ppMouseClick).Action = _
ppActionHyperlink
ActivePresentation.Slides(1).Shapes(1) _
.ActionSettings(ppMouseClick) _
.Hyperlink.Address = "http://www.cvisual.com"
```

SEE ALSO   ActionVerb

LoopUntilStopped Property

Determines whether a media clip or slide show will repeat until stopped

Description

This property can be used to make a slide show or a sound or video clip repeat. The Immediate window example expects the first shape on the first slide to be a media clip.

AVAILABLE IN VB SCRIPT

Syntax
```
playsettings.LoopUntilStopped = luFlag
```

Parameters

luFlag   Boolean. Set to True to continue cycling until a slide transition, mouse click, or another media clip begins.

Returns

Long type

Immediate Window Sample
```
ActivePresentation.Slides(1).Shapes(1). _
AnimationSettings.PlaySettings.LoopUntilStopped =
True
```

SEE ALSO   Animate, HideWhileNotPlaying

Name Property

Holds the name of the object that can be used to programmatically reference it

Description

The Name property holds the string of the name used to reference an object. Instead of using an index with a collection, the name can be used to specify the object.

AVAILABLE IN VB SCRIPT

Syntax
```
object.Name = string
```

Parameters

string   Any string conforming to the standard naming conventions

Returns

N/A

Immediate Window Sample

```
? ActivePresentation.Name
? ActivePresentation.Slides(1).Name
```

SEE ALSO   ActivePresentation

PlayOnEntry Property

Determines whether media clip is played when slide is displayed

Description

This property will make the specified media clip play when a slide is entered. The ActionVerb property can be set to determine exactly when the clip is executed.

AVAILABLE IN VB SCRIPT

Syntax

```
playsettings.PlayOnEntry = poeFlag
```

Parameters

poeFlag   Boolean. Set to True if the clip should be played on entry to the slide.

Returns

Long type

Immediate Window Sample

```
ActivePresentation.Slides(1).Shapes(1) _
.AnimationSettings.PlaySettings.PlayOnEntry = True
```

SEE ALSO   ActionVerb, Animate, EntryEffect

PresetGradient Method

Creates a gradient for the specified Fill object

Description

Use of this method creates a preset gradient in the Fill object. The style of the gradient designates its general appearance, while the gradType can be set to one of 24 different constants.

AVAILABLE IN VB SCRIPT

Syntax

```
fill.PresetGradient(style,variant, gradType)
```

Parameters

style   Use one of the following: msoGradientDiagonalDown, msoGradientDiagonalUp, msoGradientFromCenter, msoGradientFromCorner, msoGradientFromTitle, msoGradientHorizontal, or msoGradientVertical.

variant   The gradient variant that can have a value of 1 to 4.

gradType   Type of gradient. Use one of the following constants: msoGradientBrass, msoGradientCalmWater, msoGradientChrome, msoGradientChromeII, msoGradientDaybreak, msoGradientDesert, msoGradientEarlySunset, msoGradientFire, msoGradientFog, msoGradientGold, msoGradientGoldII, msoGradientHorizon, msoGradientLateSunset, msoGradientMahogany, msoGradientMoss, msoGradientNightfall, msoGradientOcean, msoGradientParchment, msoGradientPeacock, msoGradientRainbow, msoGradientRainbowII, msoGradientSapphire, msoGradientSilver, or msoGradientWheat.

Returns

N/A

Immediate Window Sample

```
ActivePresentation.Slides(1).Shapes(1).Fill _
.PresetGradient msoGradientVertical, _
1, msoGradientChrome
```

SEE ALSO PresetTextured

PresetTextEffect Property

Determines the text effect for a WordArt object

Description

WordArt objects inserted into a slide have just over 30 text effects that they may use. Unfortunately, the constants for these text effects are just the name followed by a number (msoTextEffect1...msoTextEffect30). The text effects automatically modify a number of other properties such as the fill, font, and shadow effects of the WordArt object.

The Immediate window example requires that the third shape on the first slide is a WordArt object. If it isn't, an error will occur when executing the code.

AVAILABLE IN VB SCRIPT

Syntax

```
texteffect.PresetTextEffect = effectValue
```

Parameters

effectValue Use one of the constants (msoTextEffect1... msoTextEffect30) to specify the type of effect used by WordArt.

Returns

Long type

Immediate Window Sample

```
ActivePresentation.Slides(1).Shapes(3) _
.TextEffect.PresetTextEffect = msoTextEffect15
```

SEE ALSO PresetTextured

PresetTextured Method

Creates a gradient for the specified Fill object

Description

Use of this method creates a preset texture in the Fill object. The style of the texture designates its general appearance.

AVAILABLE IN VB SCRIPT

Syntax

```
fill.PresetTextured(texture)
```

Parameters

texture   Specifies the type of texture to create for the Fill object. Use one of the following constants: msoTextureBlueTissuePaper, msoTextureBouquet, msoTextureBrownMarble, msoTextureCanvas, msoTextureCork, msoTextureDenim, msoTextureFishFossil, msoTextureGranite, msoTextureGreenMarble, msoTextureMediumWood, msoTextureNewsprint, msoTextureOak, msoTexturePaperBag, msoTexturePapyrus, msoTextureParchment, msoTexturePinkTissuePaper, msoTexturePurpleMesh, msoTextureRecycledPaper, msoTextureSand, msoTextureStationery, msoTextureWalnut, msoTextureWaterDroplets, msoTextureWhiteMarble, or msoTextureWovenMat.

Returns

Variant type

Immediate Window Sample

```
ActivePresentation.Slides(1).Shapes(1).Fill _
.PresetTextured msoTextureGreenMarble
```

SEE ALSO   PresetGradient

RGB Property

Stores the color value to be displayed by an object

Description
The RGB property is available in any of the ColorScheme objects used in PowerPoint. Change of a particular color is accomplished by setting the property to a Long RGB color value. The Immediate window example shows setting the background color of the first slide to red.

AVAILABLE IN VB SCRIPT

Syntax
```
object.RGB = color
```

Parameters
color   Long data type representing an RGB value

Returns
N/A

Immediate Window Sample
```
ActivePresentation.Slides(1). _
ColorScheme(ppBackground).RGB = RGB(255,0,0)
```

SEE ALSO   Color

Rotation Property

Contains the degrees rotation of a Shape object

Description
The Rotation property may be set in degrees to the desired angle for the object. The Immediate window example creates a label on the first slide and rotates it 45 degrees.

AVAILABLE IN VB SCRIPT

Syntax

```
object.Rotation = rotate
```

Parameters

rotate   Single value of degrees rotation

Returns

N/A

Immediate Window Sample

```
set b = ActivePresentation.Slides(1).Shapes.AddLabel _
(msoTextOrientationHorizontal,50,100,100,100) _
b.textframe.textrange.text = "Yeah"
b.rotation = 45
```

SEE ALSO   AddLabel

Run Property

Determines which macro or presentation is executed when an event occurs

Description

The Run property holds a string containing the name of the macro or presentation that is automatically executed when a particular action occurs.

AVAILABLE IN VB SCRIPT

Syntax

```
actionsetting.Run = actionName
```

Parameters

actionName   String. Name of macro or presentation to execute when event occurs.

Returns

String type

Immediate Window Sample

```
ActivePresentation.Slides(1).Shapes(1) _
.ActionSettings(ppMouseOver) _
.Action = ppActionRunMacro
ActivePresentation.Slides(1).Shapes(1) _
.ActionSettings(ppMouseOver) _
.AnimateAction = True
ActivePresentation.Slides(1).Shapes(1) _
.ActionSettings(ppMouseOver) _
.Run = "myMacro"
```

SEE ALSO   Animate

SlideRange Object

Contains references to selected slides

Description

The SlideRange object allows macro changes to be made to a series of selected slides. By making changes to the SlideRange object, changes are automatically effected in all specified slides.

AVAILABLE IN VB SCRIPT

Syntax

```
selection.SlideRange
```

Parameters

N/A

Returns

N/A

Immediate Window Sample

```
Windows(1).Selection.SlideRange _
.ColorScheme.Colors(ppBackground).RGB = RGB(255, 0,
0)
```

SEE ALSO   RGB

SlideOrientation Property

Determines orientation on screen or printed for slides

Description

The SlideOrientation property will determine the orientation of the slides. If a horizontal or vertical setting is required, these can be set. If the individual slides have differing orientations, this property will hold a mixed orientation value.

AVAILABLE IN VB SCRIPT

Syntax

```
pagesetup.SlideOrientation = orient
```

Parameters

orient   Long. This property accepts one of the following constants: msoOrientationHorizontal, msoOrientationMixed, or msoOrientationVertical.

Returns

N/A

Immediate Window Sample

```
Application.ActivePresentation.PageSetup _
.SlideOrientation = msoOrientationVertical
```

SEE ALSO   ActivePresentation

Speed Property

Determines the speed of transition to the specified slide

Description

This property governs the speed of the transition to the specified slide. Pick a transition effect that works best with the particular speed.

AVAILABLE IN VB SCRIPT

Syntax

```
slideshowtransition.Speed = transSpeed
```

Parameters

transSpeed   Long. Determines the speed of transition to the specified slide. Use one of the following constant values: ppTransitionSpeedFast, ppTransitionSpeedMedium, ppTransitionSpeedMixed, or ppTransitionSpeedSlow.

Returns

Long type

Immediate Window Sample

```
ActivePresentation.Slides(1).SlideShowTransition _
.Speed = ppTransitionSpeedSlow
```

SEE ALSO   EntryEffect

TextRange Object

Contains all of the text attached to a Shape object

Description

The TextRange object is the object that contains the Font, ParagraphFormat, and ActionSettings objects for a particular shape. The Text property of the TextRange object holds the actual text of the shape.

AVAILABLE IN VB SCRIPT

Syntax

```
shape.TextRange
```

Parameters

N/A

Returns

N/A

Immediate Window Sample

```
ActiveWindow.Selection.TextRange.Copy
```

SEE ALSO   AddLabel

ThreeD Object

Adds the 3-D appearance to Shape objects

Description

The new 3-D capabilities added to PowerPoint can be controlled through the ThreeD object. Extrusions, rotations, and perspectives can be added by varying the settings of this object.

AVAILABLE IN VB SCRIPT

Syntax

```
shape.ThreeD
```

Parameters

N/A

Returns

N/A

Immediate Window Sample

```
With ActivePresentation.Slides(1).Shapes(1).ThreeD _
.Visible = True : .Depth = 50 : _
.ExtrusionColor.RGB = RGB(255, 0, 0) : End With
```

SEE ALSO   RGB, Color

ToggleVerticalText Method

Toggles the vertical text appearance on a WordArt object

Description

This method will cause the text shown in a WordArt object to be displayed vertically. Text flow is toggled every time this method is executed. The Immediate window example requires that the third shape on the first slide is a WordArt object. If it isn't, an error will occur when executing the code.

AVAILABLE IN VB SCRIPT

Syntax
```
texteffect.ToggleVerticalText
```

Parameters
N/A

Returns
N/A

Immediate Window Sample
```
ActivePresentation.Slides(1).Shapes(3) _
.TextEffect.ToggleVerticalText
```

SEE ALSO   PresetTextEffect

TwoColorGradient Method

Creates a two-color gradient for the Fill object

Description

This method creates a two-color gradient from the Forecolor and Backcolor RGB values stored in the Fill object.

AVAILABLE IN VB SCRIPT

Syntax
```
fill.TwoColorGradient(style,variant)
```

Parameters
style   The direction/type of gradient is specified using one of the following constants: msoGradientDiagonalDown,

msoGradientDiagonalUp, msoGradientFromCenter, msoGradientFromCorner, msoGradientFromTitle, msoGradientHorizontal, or msoGradientVertical.

variant   Gradient variant that can be a value of 1 to 4.

Returns
N/A

Immediate Window Sample
```
ActivePresentation.Slides(1).Shapes(1).Fill _
    .ForeColor.RGB = RGB(255, 0, 0)
ActivePresentation.Slides(1).Shapes(1).Fill _
    .BackColor.RGB = RGB(0, 0, 0)
ActivePresentation.Slides(1).Shapes(1).Fill _
    .TwoColorGradient msoGradientHorizontal, 1
```

SEE ALSO   PresetGradient

Words Method

Returns a TextRange object that contains the specified words

Description
This method allows the extraction of particular words into a TextRange object. Use of the TextRange object will allow the manipulation of the text, style, and so on, of the specified words.

AVAILABLE IN VB SCRIPT

Syntax
```
paragraph.Words([start] [, length])
```

Parameters
start   Beginning word to be returned

length   Number of words to be returned

Returns
TextRange object

Immediate Window Sample

```
ActivePresentation.Slides(1).Shapes(1).TextFrame. _
TextRange.Paragraphs(1).Words(1, 2).Font.Bold = True
```

SEE ALSO ActivePresentation, Shape

Zoom Property

Determines the zoom percentage of the specified window

Description

This property holds the current zoom level of the window. The percentage value must be between 10 and 400, inclusive.

AVAILABLE IN VB SCRIPT

Syntax

```
window.Zoom = zoomPerc
```

Parameters

zoomPerc   Percentage of zoom from normal size of current window (10–400)

Returns

Long type

Immediate Window Sample

```
Windows(1).View.Zoom = 30
```

SEE ALSO GotoSlide, SlideOrientation

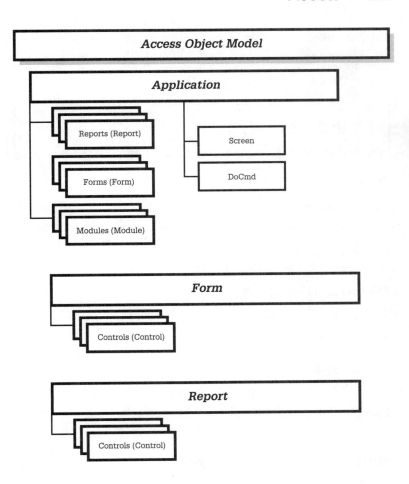

Access

Microsoft Access has only recently made the transition from the Access Basic language to including the entire VBA system. Most of the Access system can only be partially accessed. You might notice when looking at the object model that it is quite sparse. Only forms, reports, and modules are considered within the Access system. All database access occurs through the Data Access Object model.

Data Access Objects (DAO) are the general objects provided for all of the Office applications (and Visual Basic itself) to access database information. The native file format of the DAO is Microsoft Access file format, so any VBA-enabled application can read access files. The section that follows the Access section details the DAO Jet engine.

Count Property

Returns the number of objects held in the collection

Description
Use the Count property within Access to determine how many forms, reports, and so on, are held in a specific collection. The Immediate window example demonstrates how many Module objects exist in the current project.

AVAILABLE IN VB SCRIPT

Syntax
```
object.Count
```

Parameters
Long type

Returns
N/A

Immediate Window Sample
```
? Modules.Count
```

DoCmd Object

Executes specific Access commands

Description
Because the Access object model is not yet complete, there are still functions that cannot be performed through it. The DoCmd object

provides a number of capabilities to send commands to the Access program.

AVAILABLE IN VB SCRIPT

Syntax
```
DoCmd.method
```

Parameters
N/A

Returns
N/A

Immediate Window Sample
```
DoCmd.Beep
```

HourGlass Method

Changes the cursor to an hourglass or back to normal

Description
Calling the HourGlass method on the DoCmd object will change the mouse pointer to an hourglass icon showing the user that work is in progress.

AVAILABLE IN VB SCRIPT

Syntax
```
DoCmd.HourGlass flag
```

Parameters
flag   Indicates whether to set the hourglass (1) or return to the default cursor (0).

Returns
N/A

Immediate Window Sample

```
DoCmd.HourGlass 1
DoCmd.HourGlass 0
```

User Tip

Make sure to set the hourglass when an operation will take some time. It often confuses the user when the computer is processing but the cursor remains active. A general rule of thumb is that more than three seconds of processing should show the hourglass. More than 30 seconds of processing should implement some type of status display or progress bar.

Name Property

Holds the name of the object that can be used to programmatically reference it

Description

The Name property holds the string of the name used to reference an object. Instead of using an index with a collection, the name can be used to specify the object.

AVAILABLE IN VB SCRIPT

Syntax

```
object.Name = string
```

Parameters

string   Any string conforming to the standard naming conventions

Returns

N/A

Immediate Window Sample

```
? Modules(0).Name
```

Data Access Objects (DAO) Jet-engine Object Model

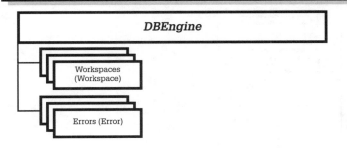

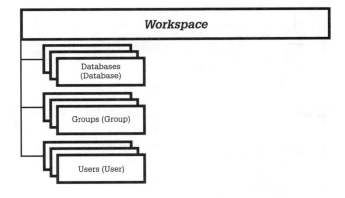

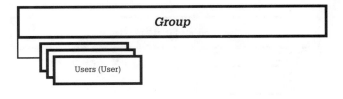

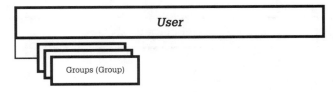

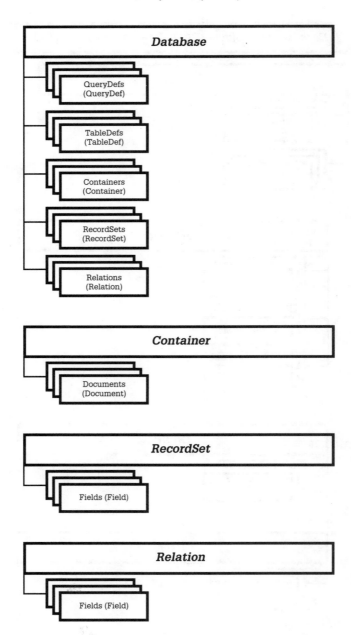

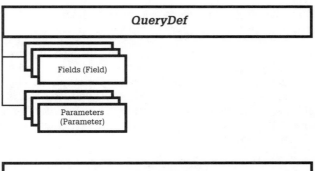

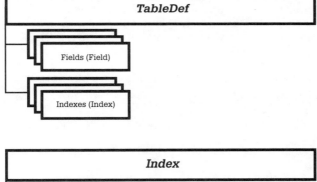

Data Access Objects (DAO) Jet Engine

Data Access Objects (DAO) are the general objects provided for all of the Office applications (and Visual Basic itself) to access database information. The native file format of the DAO is Microsoft Access file format, so any VBA-enabled application can read Access files. The actual database engine used by DAO is known as the Jet engine. You will often see information addressing optimization of the Jet engine.

The DAO format consists of a series of Workspace objects. Each Workspace is a separate security user login zone. Within the Workspace, Databases collections hold the individual Database objects that are currently open. Each Database object can contain several objects, most important of which is the Tabledefs collection. Each Tabledef object held in the collection defines the structure of individual tables stored in the database.

All of the Immediate window examples in this section were designed for use from within Microsoft Access. Some of the examples access a table named "myNames" that has two fields, ID and Name. It is necessary to create this database to run the examples without modification. If you use a different database file, be aware that some of the examples try to access these structures and will need to be modified appropriately.

There is also a Data Access Objects for ODBC. You will find the object model in the "Other Models" section. Most of the functionality is the same as the Jet model, with the primary exception of security, which is handled through the ODBC Connection object.

AddNew Method

Creates a new record in the specified table

Description
To create a new record, the AddNew method will append a record to the end of the specified recordset. The Immediate window example shows a record being added to a table named **myNames** that contains two fields. The second field is set to the name "Joe," and the Update method is called to store the new record to the table.

AVAILABLE IN VB SCRIPT

Syntax
```
object.AddNew
```

Parameters
N/A

Returns
N/A

Immediate Window Sample

```
Set a = dbEngine.Workspaces(0).Databases(0). _
Tabledefs("myNames")
a.OpenRecordset
a.AddNew
a.Field(1) = "Joe"
a.Update
```

SEE ALSO   CommitTrans

CommitTrans

Commits any records currently held in the current transaction

Description

A transaction can contain one or more changes to one or more
records. When the CommitTrans method is called, either all of the
current operations stored in the transaction are written, or a single
failure means none is written. A transaction begins with calling the
BeginTrans method; a transaction can complete with either the
CommitTrans or RollBack methods.

AVAILABLE IN VB SCRIPT

Syntax

```
dbEngine.CommitTrans
```

Parameters

N/A

Returns

N/A

Immediate Window Sample

N/A

SEE ALSO   BeginTrans, RollBack

CompactDatabase

Compacts the specified database and stores it in the new file

Description
When records are deleted from a database, they are not truly expunged from the current data file, but merely marked as deleted. CompactDatabase removes these records and other unneeded data.

AVAILABLE IN VB SCRIPT

Syntax
```
dbEngine.CompactDatabase source$ Dest$ [, Locale$ [,
options&]]
```

Parameters
source$ Any valid path and filename that points to the source file

Dest$ Any valid path and filename that points to the destination file

Returns
N/A

Immediate Window Sample
```
dbEngine.CompactDatabase "start.mdb" "end.mdb"
```

SEE ALSO   RepairDatabase

Database Object

Contains all of the tables and queries for a database

Description
The Database object is held in a collection of Databases that are all of the open databases within a workspace. The Immediate window example displays the name of the first Database object in the

collection. If the object is an Access file, the name displayed is a complete path and filename.

AVAILABLE IN VB SCRIPT

Syntax
N/A

Parameters
N/A

Returns
N/A

Immediate Window Sample
```
? dbEngine.Workspaces(0).Databases.Count
? dbEngine.Workspaces(0).Databases(0).Name
```

SEE ALSO   Workspace, Tabledef

Delete Method

Deletes an object from a collection

Description
The Delete method on many of the Access objects allows you to remove an object (such as a database, table, query, field, and so on) from a collection. The Immediate window example removes one of the fields from the myNames table.

AVAILABLE IN VB SCRIPT

Syntax
```
object.Delete(object)
```

Parameters
object   May be either the ordinal index number or the name of the object to be removed

Returns

N/A

Immediate Window Sample

```
Set a = dbEngine.Workspaces(0).Databases(0). _
Tabledefs("myNames")
a.Fields.Delete("name")
```

SEE ALSO Database object

Field Object

Holds the actual structure information for a particular field within a table

Description

The Field object can be used to reference either the field within the Table object that it represents, or the data stored within the data field itself. The Immediate window example displays all of the fields contained in the myName table.

AVAILABLE IN VB SCRIPT

Syntax

N/A

Parameters

N/A

Returns

N/A

Immediate Window Sample

```
Set a = dbEngine.Workspaces(0).Databases(0). _
Tabledefs("myNames")
? a.Fields.count
for i = 0 to a.Fields.Count -1 : ? a.Fields(i).Name :
Next i
```

SEE ALSO AddNew, Database object

Refresh Method

Requeries the specified structure for updated information

Description
The Refresh method can be used on databases to locate new tables, on tables to locate new fields, or on recordsets to access new records that have been added.

AVAILABLE IN VB SCRIPT

Syntax
```
object.Refresh
```

Parameters
N/A

Returns
N/A

Immediate Window Sample
```
Set a = dbEngine.Workspaces(0).Databases(0). _
Tabledefs("myNames")
a.Fields.Refresh
```

SEE ALSO   Database object

RepairDatabase Method

Repairs any damage to the database file

Description
Database files can become corrupted by power failures, operating system crashes, or other disasters. The RepairDatabase method will review the entire database and find and repair any aberrations.

AVAILABLE IN VB SCRIPT

Syntax
```
dbEngine.RepairDatabase(filename$)
```

Parameters
filename$ Any valid path and filename to an Access database

Returns
N/A

Immediate Window Sample
```
dbEngine.RepairDatabase "c:\bad.mbd"
```

SEE ALSO   CompactDatabase

RollBack Method

Aborts any operations currently held in the transaction

Description
A transaction begun with the BeginTrans method can be revoked with the RollBack method. This may be caused by an error while writing one of the records or by any other abort reason.

Syntax
```
dbEngine.RollBack
```

Parameters
N/A

Returns
N/A

Immediate Window Sample
N/A

SEE ALSO   BeginTrans, CommitTrans

Tabledef Object

Holds the structure and data of a table

Description
The Tabledef object is stored within the Tabledefs collection for all of the tables within a particular database. The Immediate window example shows obtaining the count and name of the Tabledefs of the collection. Also demonstrated is the display of the DateCreated property of a table named myNames.

AVAILABLE IN VB SCRIPT

Syntax
N/A

Parameters
N/A

Returns
N/A

Immediate Window Sample
```
? dbEngine.Workspaces(0).Databases(0).Tabledefs.count
? DbEngine.Workspaces(0).Databases(0). _
Tabledefs(0).Name
? DbEngine.Workspaces(0).Databases(0). _
Tabledefs("myNames").DateCreated
```

SEE ALSO   Database

Workspace Object

Object that holds the current database workspaces

Description
Each Workspace has particular security privileges for access to a Database held within the Databases collection.

AVAILABLE IN VB SCRIPT

Syntax
N/A

Parameters
N/A

Returns
N/A

Immediate Window Sample
```
? dbEngine.Workspaces.Count
```

SEE ALSO   Database, Tabledef

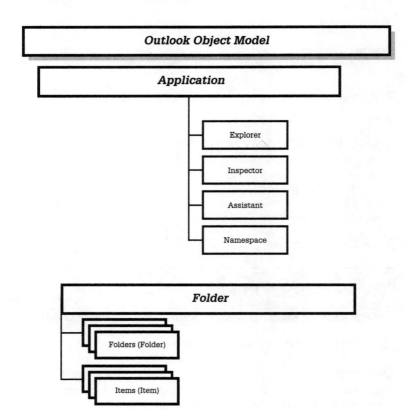

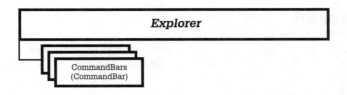

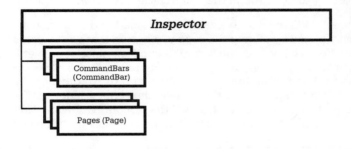

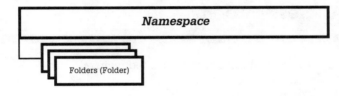

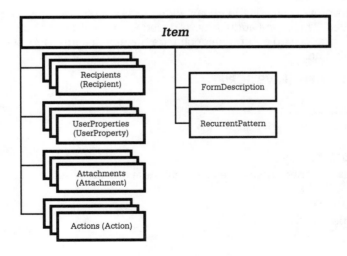

Outlook

Microsoft Outlook includes the VB Script language instead of VBA. Therefore, it uses a custom VB Script environment that is not as robust as those included with the other Office applications. All code is placed within the tabbed pages of an Item form, so accessing objects is done through the hierarchical chain from that form.

The Immediate window examples provided in this section are most easily tested by adding the code to a button that you've placed on a modified tab page. In the Scripting window, place code that begins with "Sub myButton_Click()", where myButton is the name of the button. End the subroutine definition with the traditional "End Sub". If you simply place this code in the script window and select the Run menu command, many of the samples will work. However, all of the samples work when included in a button Click event.

Address Property

Holds the e-mail address of the specified recipient

Description

This property holds the e-mail address after a recipient has been added. The e-mail address is retrieved from the Address book. Use this property to determine or change the e-mail address for the mail item.

AVAILABLE IN VB SCRIPT

Syntax

```
recipient.Address = email
```

Parameters

email   String. Holds specified mail item e-mail address.

Returns

Variant type

Immediate Window Sample

```
Set myItem = Application.CreateItem(0) ' olMailItem
Set myRecipient = myItem.Recipients.Add "Dan Rahmel"
MsgBox myRecipient.Address
```

SEE ALSO   CreateItem

AllDayEvent Property

Determines whether event is all day or at a specific time

Description

This property determines whether the event is all day. If this property is set to True, the specific time property values of this appointment item are ignored.

AVAILABLE IN VB SCRIPT

Syntax

```
item.AllDayEvent = alldayFlag
```

Parameters

alldayFlag   Boolean. Set to True if event is all day.

Returns

Long type

Immediate Window Sample

```
Set myItem = Application.CreateItem(1) _
' olAppointmentItem
myItem.AllDayEvent = True
```

SEE ALSO   CreateItem, ClearRecurrencePattern

Body Property

Contains the body text of an item

Description

This property contains the plain text (or clear text) of an item such as a mail message or a post. Change the body of the item by changing the value of this property.

AVAILABLE IN VB SCRIPT

Syntax

```
item.Body = text
```

Parameters

text   String. Body text of message.

Returns

String type

Immediate Window Sample

```
Set myItem = Application.CreateItem(0) ' olMailItem
myItem.Body = "Welcome to VB Script!"
```

SEE ALSO   CreateItem, Address

ClearRecurrencePattern Method

Clears the recurrence pattern for an appointment or task

Description

Calling this method sets the single occurrence state of a task or appointment.

AVAILABLE IN VB SCRIPT

Syntax

```
appointment.ClearRecurrencePattern
```

Parameters

N/A

Returns

N/A

Immediate Window Sample

```
myApptment.ClearRecurrencePattern
```

SEE ALSO   AllDayEvent

Controls Property

Provides access to controls stored on a modified tab

Description

Each tab that is visible can have controls such as Text Box, List Box, Check Box, Options, and so on. The Controls property provides access to the Controls collection for a tab.

AVAILABLE IN VB SCRIPT

Syntax

```
object.Controls
```

Parameters

N/A

Returns

N/A

Immediate Window Sample

```
Set myCtls = Item.GetInspector. _
ModifiedFormPages("(P.1)").Controls
If myCtls("chkMyBox") Then MsgBox "Checked"
```

SEE ALSO   GetInspector

Count Property

Returns the number of items in collection

Description

To determine the number of objects in a collection, access the Count property. Although the For...Next loop can be used with the Count property, instead use the For...Each loop to move through an object collection.

AVAILABLE IN VB SCRIPT

Syntax

```
collection.Count
```

Parameters

N/A

Returns

Long type

Immediate Window Sample

```
MsgBox Folders.Count
```

SEE ALSO   GetDefaultFolder

CreateItem Method

Creates a new Outlook item

Description

To create a new contact, note, or other Outlook item, the CreateItem method will add it to the current file.

AVAILABLE IN VB SCRIPT

Syntax

```
Set object = Application.CreateItem(itmType)
```

Parameters

itmType   Type of new item to insert

Returns

Object type

Immediate Window Sample

```
Set newContact = Application.CreateItem(4) ' Contact
Set newNote = Application.CreateItem(5) ' Note
```

SEE ALSO   Controls

CreateObject Method

Creates an object reference based on the class or class ID specified

Description

This method instantiates an OLE Automation object from the specified class or class ID.

AVAILABLE IN VB SCRIPT

Syntax

```
Set object = CreateObject(class)
```

Parameters

class   Class identified by string that contains either the class name or the class ID

Returns

Object type

Immediate Window Sample

```
Set myObject = CreateObject("Outlook.Application")
Set nms = myObject.GetNameSpace("MAPI")
```

SEE ALSO   CreateItem

CurrentFolder Property

Determines the current folder shown in the Explorer

Description

The CurrentFolder property holds the category of folder that is selected for the user to view.

AVAILABLE IN VB SCRIPT

Syntax

```
explorer.CurrentFolder = folderRef
```

Parameters

folderRef   Reference to the folder that is shown in the Explorer view

Returns

MAPIFolder type

Immediate Window Sample

```
Set Application.ActiveExplorer.CurrentFolder = _
    olNameSpace.GetDefaultFolder(olFolderCalendar)
```

SEE ALSO   GetNameSpace

CurrentUser Property

Holds the identification of the user currently logged into Outlook

Description

Accessing the CurrentUser property will provide the name of the currently logged-in user. Using the property can allow recording of who is accessing the item.

AVAILABLE IN VB SCRIPT

Syntax

```
namespace.CurrentUser
```

Parameters

N/A

Returns

N/A

Immediate Window Sample

```
Set nms = Application.GetNameSpace("MAPI")
MsgBox nms.CurrentUser
```

SEE ALSO GetNameSpace

Display Method

Displays the specified item

Description

Calling the Display method will make an item visible. When a new item is created, the item is invisible by default. An item can be a Contact sheet, a Meeting, an Email entry, or any other Outlook form-based object.

AVAILABLE IN VB SCRIPT

Syntax

```
object.Display
```

Parameters

N/A

Returns

N/A

Immediate Window Sample

```
Set newContact = Application.CreateItem(4)
newContact.Display
```

SEE ALSO CreateItem, DisplayName

DisplayName Property

Determines the caption below the attachment

Description

For an attachment to a piece of mail, the DisplayName property may be used to set it to something other than the actual filename. Therefore, even if you're sending to a system using the eight-character DOS file convention, the name on the attachment can be descriptive.

AVAILABLE IN VB SCRIPT

Syntax

```
attach.DisplayName = name
```

Parameters

name   String. Contains the name that will be displayed on the attachment when item is viewed.

Returns

String type

Immediate Window Sample

```
Set myItem = Application.CreateItem(0)  ' olMailItem
Set myAttachments = myItem.Attachments
Set myAttach = myAttachments.Add "C:\test.xls"
myAttach.DisplayName = "This is a test"
```

SEE ALSO   CreateItem, Body

Duration Property

Determines the duration in minutes of the appointment

Description
Sets the duration of an appointment or journal entry in minutes. This property is also used within appointments for the recurrence pattern.

AVAILABLE IN VB SCRIPT

Syntax
```
item.Duration = minutes
```

Parameters
minutes   Long. Duration in minutes.

Returns
Long type

Immediate Window Sample
```
Set myItem = Application.CreateItem(1) _
' olAppointmentItem
myItem.Duration = 48 * 60 ' 2 days = 48 hrs * 60 min
```

SEE ALSO   AllDayEvent, ClearRecurrencePattern

FileAs Property

Contains the keyword string when a contact is filed

Description
This property is automatically initialized when contact is first created. Use the property to set or retrieve the default keyword string.

AVAILABLE IN VB SCRIPT

Syntax
```
item.FileAs = fileStr
```

Parameters
fileStr   String. Default keyword string assigned to contact.

Returns
String type

Immediate Window Sample
```
Set myItem = Application.CreateItem(2) _
' olContactItem
myItem.FileAs = "DP artist"
```

SEE ALSO   CreateItem, DisplayName

GetDefaultFolder Method

Provides a reference to one of the default folders

Description
Complete access to the items within a folder is possible once an object reference to the folder itself has been obtained.

AVAILABLE IN VB SCRIPT

Syntax
```
Set myObject = object.GetDefaultFolder(fnum)
```

Parameters
fnum   Contains the index number of the desired folder

Returns
Object type

Immediate Window Sample
```
Set myContacts = Application. _
GetNameSpace("MAPI").GetDefaultFolder(10)
```

SEE ALSO   GetNameSpace

GetInspector Property

Provides the top-level Inspector object

Description
The Inspector is required for access to many parts of the Outlook system. Using the GetInspector property, code on an Item form can obtain a reference.

AVAILABLE IN VB SCRIPT

Syntax
```
Set myObject = object.GetInspector
```

Parameters
object   Valid Item object

Returns
Object type

Immediate Window Sample
```
Set a = myItem.GetInspector
```

SEE ALSO   CreateItem

GetNameSpace Method

Returns the object reference to the NameSpace object of the type specified

Description
This method returns the reference from the root data source. The object can be used to retrieve information from the folders, to get user information, and to access other data sources. Currently, only the "MAPI" name space type is supported.

AVAILABLE IN VB SCRIPT

Syntax
```
Set object = GetNameSpace(type)
```

Parameters
type String. Name space type to return object reference.

Returns
String type

Immediate Window Sample
```
Set nms = Application.GetNameSpace("MAPI")
```

SEE ALSO CreateItem, GetDefaultFolder

HideFormPage Method

Hides a specified form page

Description
This method sets the form page to be hidden from the Inspector.
The Immediate window example requires a page named MyPage
to exist in the item.

AVAILABLE IN VB SCRIPT

Syntax
```
inspector.HideFormPage(pageName)
```

Parameters
pageName String. Name of page to be hidden.

Returns
String type

Immediate Window Sample
```
Application.GetInspector.HideFormPage("MyPage")
```

SEE ALSO GetInspector, ShowFormPage

Importance Property

Determines the importance of an Outlook item

Description
This property contains the importance level (low, normal, or high) of an item. This property is available to every item type.

AVAILABLE IN VB SCRIPT

Syntax
```
item.Importance = level
```

Parameters
level   Long. The level can be set to one of three values: olImportanceLow (0), olImportanceNormal (1), and olImportanceHigh (2).

Returns
Long type

Immediate Window Sample
```
Set myItem = Application.CreateItem(1) _
' olAppointmentItem
myItem.Importance = 2 ' olImportanceHigh
```

SEE ALSO   AllDayEvent, ClearRecurrencePattern, CreateItem, Duration

MeetingStatus Property

Determines the meeting status of an Appointment item

Description
The MeetingStatus property can determine the status of a meeting and make the MeetingRequestItem available to the appointment.

AVAILABLE IN VB SCRIPT

Syntax
```
item.MeetingStatus = meetType
```

Parameters
meetType   Long. The type can be set to one of three values: olMeeting (1), olMeetingCanceled (5), olMeetingReceived (3), or olNonMeeting (0).

Returns
Long type

Immediate Window Sample
```
Set myItem = Application.CreateItem(1) _
' olAppointmentItem
myItem.MeetingStatus = 1 ' olMeeting
```

SEE ALSO   AllDayEvent, ClearRecurrencePattern, CreateItem, Duration

ModifiedFormPages Property

Holds reference to any of the user-modifiable tabs collection

Description
In Outlook, all form construction occurs on the additional hidden tabs of an Item object. This property provides a reference to enable access to items on the modified pages.

AVAILABLE IN VB SCRIPT

Syntax
```
object.ModifiedFormPages
```

Parameters
N/A

Returns
N/A

Immediate Window Sample

```
Set myPages = Item.GetInspector.ModifiedFormPages
```

SEE ALSO   CreateItem, GetInspector

ResponseState Property

Determines the status of a task request

Description

This property can be used to quickly set or determine information on the overall status of a task request. Using this property with an automated routine can presort incoming tasks.

AVAILABLE IN VB SCRIPT

Syntax

```
item.ResponseState = state
```

Parameters

state   Long. Holds the current state of the task that is one of these values: olTaskAccept (2), olTaskAssign (1), olTaskDecline (3), or olTaskSimple (0).

Returns

Long type

Immediate Window Sample

```
Set myItem = Application.CreateItem(3)  ' olTaskItem
myItem.ResponseState = 1 ' TaskAssign
```

SEE ALSO   CreateItem, Save

Save Method

Stores any changes in the form fields to the Outlook database

Description

Programmatically or through user interaction, changes that occur to the Outlook fields are not automatically stored to the file. Calling the Save method will update any changes.

AVAILABLE IN VB SCRIPT

Syntax

```
object.Save
```

Parameters

object   Any valid Item object.

Returns

N/A

Immediate Window Sample

```
Item.Save
```

SEE ALSO   CreateItem, Duration, ResponseState

Sensitivity Property

Determines the sensitivity or confidentiality of an item

Description

The Sensitivity property can be set to make an item Normal, Personal, Private, or Confidential.

AVAILABLE IN VB SCRIPT

Syntax

```
item.Sensitivity = value
```

Parameters

value   Long. The sensitivity is determined by one of the following values: olConfidential (3), olNormal (0), olPersonal (1), or olPrivate (2).

Returns
Long type

Immediate Window Sample
```
Set myItem = Application.CreateItem(1) _
' olAppointmentItem
myItem.Sensitivity = 3 ' olConfidential
```

SEE ALSO   CreateItem, ResponseState

SetCurrentPage Method

Sets the title of the current tabbed page on the Item

Description
Items on a tabbed Outlook form do not have a traditional Name property, but must be referenced by the tab caption. This method sets the caption for the current tab.

AVAILABLE IN VB SCRIPT

Syntax
```
object.SetCurrentPage = titleString
```

Parameters
titleString   Any valid page name

Returns
N/A

Immediate Window Sample
```
Item.GetInspector.SetCurrentPage = "myPageTitle"
```

SEE ALSO   GetInspector, HideFormPage, ShowFormPage

ShowFormPage Method

Shows a specified form page

Description

This method sets the form page to be shown by the Inspector. The Immediate window example requires a page named MyPage to exist in the item.

AVAILABLE IN VB SCRIPT

Syntax

```
inspector.ShowFormPage(pageName)
```

Parameters

pageName   String. Name of page to be hidden.

Returns

String type

Immediate Window Sample

```
Application.GetInspector.ShowFormPage("MyPage")
```

SEE ALSO   GetInspector, HideFormPage

UserProperties Collection

Holds all of the fields or properties added by a user

Description

All of the normal fields are referenced by simply using the dot (.) command. However, properties/fields added by the user are stored in the UserProperties collection and must be referenced through it.

AVAILABLE IN VB SCRIPT

Syntax

```
item.UserProperties(propName)
```

Parameters

propName   String. Valid property name.

Returns

Variant type

Immediate Window Sample

```
MsgBox Item.UserProperties("Custom1").Value
```

SEE ALSO   Controls, CreateItem

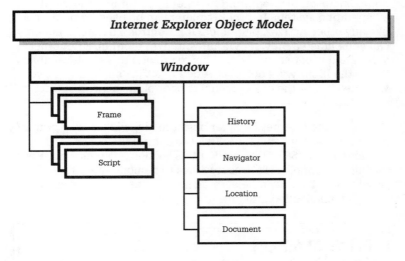

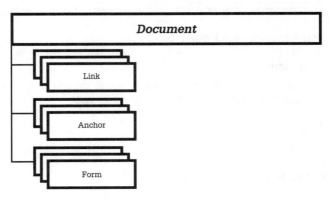

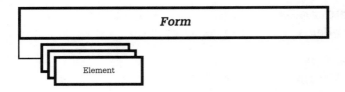

Internet Explorer

The Internet Explorer object model has a more important use than the potential VB Script code that can be embedded into an HTML page. Microsoft is integrating Internet Explorer into the Windows 98 operating system. Internet Explorer can be used by programs like any other ActiveX plug-in or OLE Control. Therefore, not only can you embed a browser within your own programs, but other software developers also are likely to provide this same capability. When the IE browser object is added to a VBA environment, you will need to use the object model to control the actions of the embedded browser.

Currently, the Internet Explorer object model will be used primarily by Web page developers. VB Script to control the objects is contained in a <SCRIPT> tag. For this section, examples have been included as simple HTML source files to demonstrate the capabilities. These can be entered into any text editor, such as Notepad, and loaded into Internet Explorer.

Back Method

Moves the browser back one link

Description
Use the Back method (there is also a Forward method available) to move within the History list of the current browser.

Syntax
`History.Back`

Parameters
N/A

Returns

N/A

HTML Code Sample

```
<HTML>
<BODY>
<FORM NAME="myForm">
        String: <INPUT NAME="myString" VALUE=""
        MAXLENGTH="50" SIZE=50>
        <INPUT TYPE="BUTTON" VALUE="Go"
        NAME="cmdGo">
</FORM>

<SCRIPT LANGUAGE="VBScript">
Sub cmdGo_OnClick
    History.Back
End Sub
</SCRIPT>
</BODY>
</HTML>
```

SEE ALSO   Document

Document Object

This object is the central HTML document

Description

The Document object holds all of the HTML, form, ActiveX, Java, and other objects for the current page. The sample code is a simple HTML page that uses VB Script and the Write method of the Document object to write text to the page text.

Syntax

N/A

Parameters

N/A

Returns

N/A

HTML Code Sample

```
<HTML>
<SCRIPT LANGUAGE="VBScript">
<!--
    myGreeting = "Hello World<P>"
    Document.Write myGreeting
-->
</SCRIPT>
</HTML><BR>
```

SEE ALSO   Back, HRef

HRef Property

The HRef property holds the currently browsed URL location

Description

Examining this property will allow a program to determine the
current URL. Setting the property will change the viewed site to
the new URL.

Syntax

```
Location.HRef = string
```

Parameters

string   Required. Complete URL to a location.

Returns

N/A

HTML Code Sample

```
<HTML>
<BODY>
<FORM NAME="myForm">
        String: <INPUT NAME="myString" VALUE=""
        MAXLENGTH="50" SIZE=50>
        <INPUT TYPE="BUTTON" VALUE="Go"
```

```
        NAME="cmdGo">
</FORM>

<SCRIPT LANGUAGE="VBScript">
Sub cmdGo_OnClick
    Dim curForm
    Set curForm=Document.Forms.item(0)
    Location.HRef = curForm.myString.Value
End Sub
</SCRIPT>
</BODY>
</HTML>
```

User Tip
Make sure the HRef property is set to a complete URL (that is, http://...). If the URL is incomplete, an error won't be generated. The browser will simply not move to the new location.

SEE ALSO   Document, Back

Item Method

Returns a reference to an item stored on the HTML page

Description
Use the Item method to gain references to objects that are active on the current page. The sample code demonstrates referencing a Form object on the page and retrieving the value from the input text box.

Syntax
```
Set myObject = object.Item(refNum)
```

Parameters
refNum   The reference number of the object within the HTML page

Returns
Object type

HTML Code Sample

```
<HTML>
<BODY>
<FORM NAME="myForm">
        String: <INPUT NAME="myString" VALUE=""
        MAXLENGTH="50" SIZE=50>
        <INPUT TYPE="BUTTON" VALUE="Go"
        NAME="cmdGo">
</FORM>

<SCRIPT LANGUAGE="VBScript">
Sub cmdGo_OnClick
    Dim curForm
    Set curForm=Document.Forms.item(0)
    MsgBox "You entered: " + curForm.myString.Value
End Sub
</SCRIPT>
</BODY>
</HTML><BR>
```

SEE ALSO   Document, Submit

Submit Method

Sends the data entered into the user form

Description

By trapping the Submit method, as shown in the sample code, the contents of submitted information can be checked. If the data is valid, calling the Submit method manually will actually activate the Submit operation.

Syntax

`object.Submit`

Parameters

N/A

Returns

N/A

HTML Code Sample

```
<HTML>
<BODY>
<FORM NAME="myForm">
        String: <INPUT NAME="myString" VALUE=""
        MAXLENGTH="50" SIZE=50>
        <INPUT TYPE="BUTTON" VALUE="Go"
        NAME="cmdGo">
</FORM>

<SCRIPT LANGUAGE="VBScript">
Sub cmdGo_OnClick
    Dim curForm
    Set curForm=Document.Forms.item(0)
    If RTrim(curForm.myString.Value)="" then
        MsgBox "Empty.", 16, "Bad."
    Else
        MsgBox "Full", 32, "OK."
        curForm.Submit
    End if
End Sub
</SCRIPT>
</BODY>
</HTML><BR>
```

SEE ALSO   Document, Item

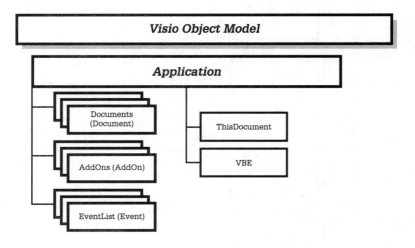

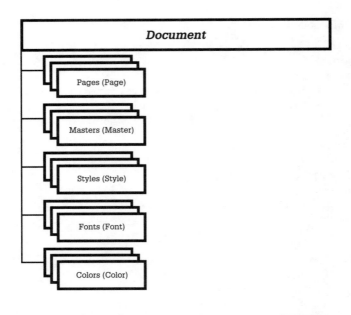

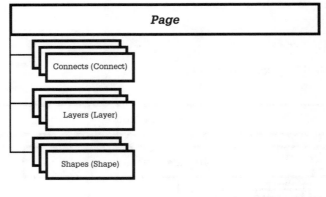

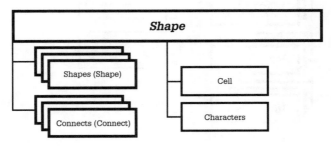

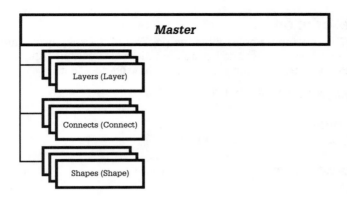

Visio

The Visio drag-and-drop drawing application was one of the first
popular third-party applications to include complete VBA
integration. In addition to the most recent versions featuring the
VBA interface, the complete application has been broken down
into OLE Automation objects. These objects will allow you to
construct a Visio diagram from within another VBA application.

Therefore, a program could be created to construct a diagram from
the data contained in an Excel spreadsheet. Or actual layout pages
could be constructed to summarize a PowerPoint presentation. Or
all of the current employees of an organization could be taken from
an Outlook category and constructed within a diagram for easy
organization chart layout.

Simple object manipulation of the Visio object model is extremely
easy because the interface is straightforward. For more complex
access, such as that required to manipulate Visio's advanced
AutoCAD features, see the Visio developer Web site
(**http://www.visio.com/devweb**).

Document Object

Visio document that holds both the document and the proper
references to the foundation template

Description

A Visio document holds all of the pages and the shapes contained within those pages. The Document object also contains the references to the templates used within the document.

AVAILABLE IN VB SCRIPT

Syntax

```
[Application.] Document
```

Parameters

N/A

Returns

N/A

Immediate Window Sample

```
Set myDocument = Documents("basic.vss")
```

SEE ALSO   Drop, Text

Drop Method

Moves a drag-and-drop shape onto the document

Description

Visio's visual style of drawing construction requires programming as if the user were constructing the diagram. Using the Drop method will drag and drop a shape from one of the templates and place it in the document.

AVAILABLE IN VB SCRIPT

Syntax

```
document.Drop(master,x,y)
```

Parameters

master   Object reference to a master shape for placement in the document

x, y   The x and y coordinates to place the shape

Returns
Variant type

Immediate Window Sample
```
Set myDocument = Documents("basic.vss")
Set master = myDocument.Masters("Star 5")
Set shape = myDocument.Drop(master, 3, 2)
```

SEE ALSO   Document, Text

Save Method

Saves changes to existing file

Description
Use the Save method to write changes made to a document to the disk (the SaveAs method is also available). If the file has not been previously saved, the user will be presented with a Save As dialog box.

AVAILABLE IN VB SCRIPT

Syntax
```
document.Save
```

Parameters
N/A

Returns
String type

Immediate Window Sample
```
Set myDocument = Documents("basic.vss")
myDocument.Save
```

SEE ALSO   Document, SaveAs

SaveAs Method

Saves changes to specified filename

Description
Use the SaveAs method to write changes made to a document to the disk (the Save method is also available) or to save a current document under a new filename.

AVAILABLE IN VB SCRIPT

Syntax
```
document.SaveAs fileName
```

Parameters
fileName   String. Fully qualified path and filename to store the file.

Returns
String type

Immediate Window Sample
```
Set myDocument = Documents("basic.vss")
myDocument.SaveAs "c:\test.vsd"
```

SEE ALSO   Document, Save

Text Property

Determines the text that will be displayed inside the object

Description
Every Visio shape contains the ability to display text. This property will contain the text for each shape and connector.

AVAILABLE IN VB SCRIPT

Syntax

```
shape.Text = text
```

Parameters

text   String. Visible text stored for the shape.

Returns

String type

Immediate Window Sample

```
Set myDocument = Documents("basic.vss")
Set master = myDocument.Masters("Star 5")
Set shape = myDocument.Drop(master, 3, 2)
shape.Text = "My First Object"
```

SEE ALSO   Document, Drop

Other Object Models

The following object models are handy to have for reference, but you may not need them every day. Remember to use the Object Browser (F2 from the VBA environment) to examine the exact methods and properties available for any object or collection. If you have the proper help file installed (the system will tell you), you can select a property or method and press the F1 key to show the help related to that item that is selected in the Object Browser.

If the object set you need does not appear in the Object Browser (for example, you need access to the Word object model while in the Excel environment), you probably haven't added it to the available references. Select the References option to select the desired object models. The References option appears under different menus in different applications, but appears under the Tools menu in VBA. Simply place a check box to the left of any object model you need to examine. The objects will now appear in the Object Browser.

If you cannot locate the object set you need in the list, it may not be registered on your system. Make sure you have the application installed. If you still cannot locate it, you may just be overlooking it in the list. Some companies, like Microsoft, usually place the company name before the entry (for example, Microsoft Outlook Object Library), but not always. Initials are often used as well ("IE" stands for "Internet Explorer"). Carefully check the list for the item that you need.

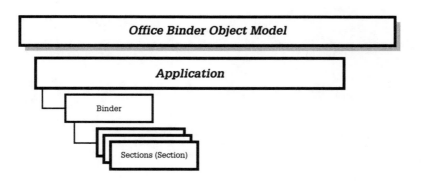

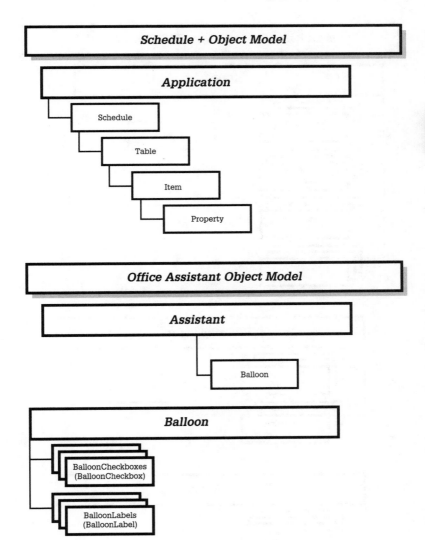

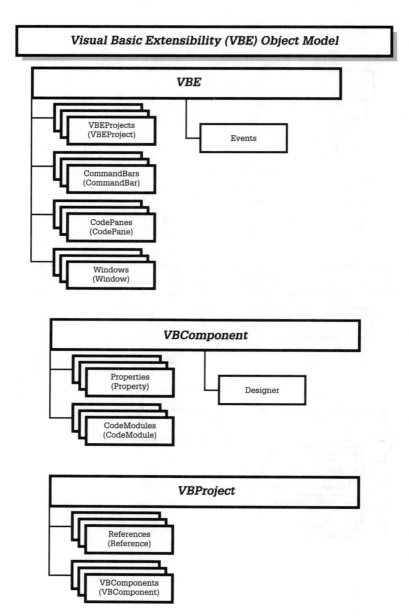

Microsoft Project Object Model

Application

- Projects (Project)
- Windows (Window)
- Cell
- Selection

3

Project

- Resources (Resource)
- Calendars (Calendar)
- Tasks (Task)
- List

Resource

- Assignments (Assignment)
- Calendar

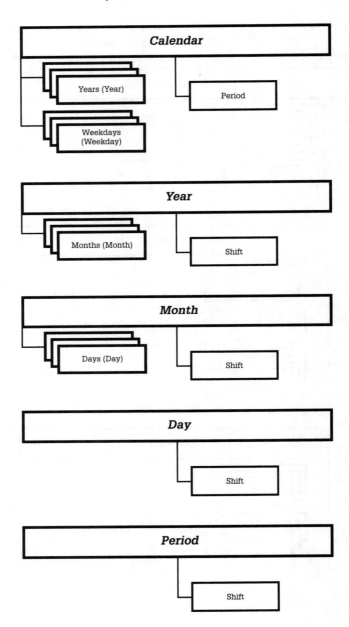

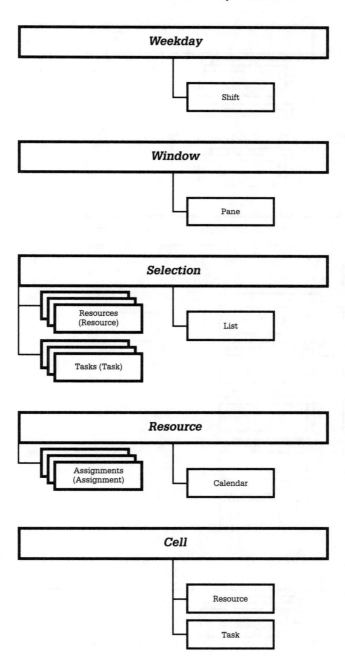

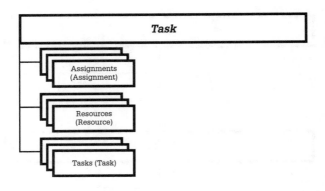

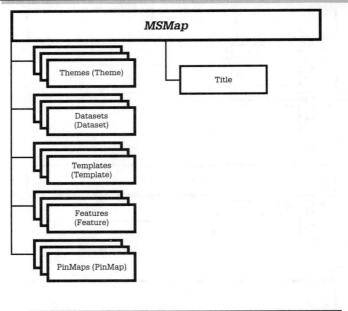

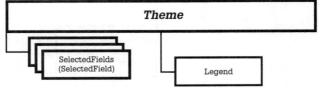

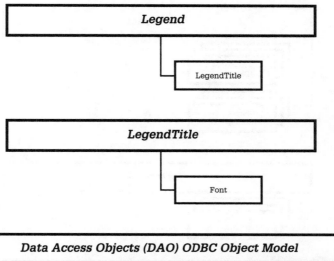

Data Access Objects (DAO) ODBC Object Model

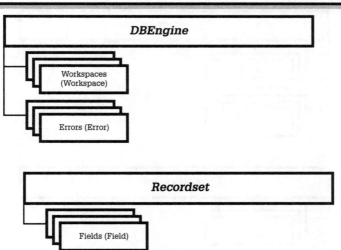

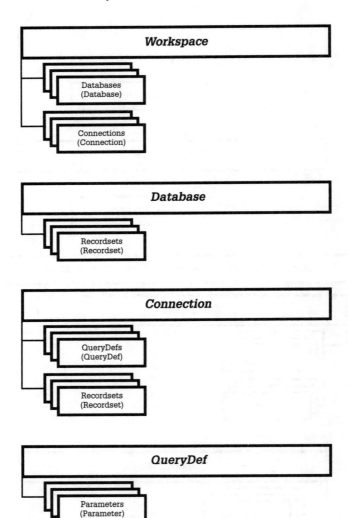